CONTENTS

CKLIST

LIBRARY

DING DESIGN

NSIDERATIONS

WILLIAM W. SANNWALD

AMERICAN LIBRARY ASSOCIATION
Chicago and London
2001

Cover and text design by Dianne M. Rooney

Composition by ALA Editions in Palatino and Syntax using QuarkXpress 4.11 for the Power Macintosh 7100/66

Printed on 50-pound white offset, a pH-neutral stock, and bound in 10-point cover stock by Batson Printing

The paper used in this publication meets the minimum requirements of American National Standard for Information Sciences—Permanence of Paper for Printed Library Materials, ANSI Z39. 48-1992.♾

Library of Congress Cataloging-in-Publication Data

Checklist of library building design considerations / [edited by] William W.
    Sannwald.—4th ed.
        p.   cm.
    "For the Architecture of Public Libraries Committee, LAMA Buildings and Equipment Section."
    Includes bibliographical references.
    ISBN 0-8389-3506-0
    1. Library architecture—United States.   I. Sannwald, William W.
II. Library Administration and Management Association. Buildings & Equipment Section. Architecture for Public Libraries Committee.

Z679.2.U54C44 2001
727'.8—dc21   00-052164

Printed in the United States of America.

05 04 03 02 01   5 4 3 2 1

Contents

PREFACE

This fourth edition of the *Checklist of Library Building Design Considerations* is published to accomplish a number of goals:

- To assist librarians, architects, administrators, and other members of a building design team in programming library spaces.

- To serve as a guide during the various stages of the design process in order to make sure that all needed spaces and functions are included in the library design.

- To enable the evaluation of existing library spaces as part of a library's Needs Assessment Process.

- To provide data and support to the library in their presentations to governing authorities and stakeholder groups.

In the *Checklist*, questions are asked concerning almost every aspect of space and function in a library building. The purpose of the questions is to make sure that the building design team in the evaluation and programming of spaces overlooks no element of the building. While the list of questions is probably not exhaustive, answering the questions in this document should ensure that no major design elements have been overlooked.

The *Checklist* is a valuable tool for programming and planning existing and potential library buildings. Most of the basic areas listed in the *Checklist* apply to college and university, public, school, and special libraries. It should be relatively easy to adapt the *Checklist* to meet the requirements of almost any type of library.

The first edition was adapted from a checklist produced by doctoral students in the School of Library and Information Studies at Texas Woman's University in Denton. The fourth edition has some new sections including a way to determine the adequacies of existing library facilities, and how to determine how much space is required in a new building. Other new sections include sustainable design or green architecture, alternatives to new construction, joint use considerations, and the institutional planning team. Also for the first time are new sections on young adults, remote storage, moving libraries, occupancy, and post-occupancy evaluation. All sections in the fourth edition have been revised including an extensive revision of the children's and technology sections.

Thanks go to the following people who helped me with preparing the fourth edition of the *Checklist*. Shannon Kekos from my staff proofed and formatted the publication. Thanks also to two students at the San Jose State University School of Library and Information Science, Cynthia Shutler and Jill Woolums, who researched some of the new topics. Special thanks also to Aditi Shah, a graduate student at the New School of Architecture in San Diego, and the dean of the school, Michael Stepner, FAIA.

This publication should be viewed as a living document, and all comments and additions suggested for future editions are welcome. Please send them to:

San Diego Public Library
820 E Street
San Diego, CA 92101-6478

WILLIAM W. SANNWALD

Building Planning and Architecture

	YES	NO	N/A

A. Indicators of Dissatisfaction with Existing Facilities

1. Does the existing building hinder the delivery of good service?

   Comments: _____

   _____

2. Is there enough room for the products and services the library offers?

   Comments: _____

   _____

3. In order to accommodate collection growth, have seats been exchanged for stacks?

   Comments: _____

   _____

4. Is the atmosphere of the library pleasing for customers and staff?

   Comments: _____

   _____

5. Has the population served by the library increased?

   Comments: _____

   _____

	YES	NO	N/A

6. Have the demographics of the population served
    by the library changed?

    Comments: _____

    _____

7. Has the emphasis of the products and services
    offered by the library changed?

    Comments: _____

    _____

8. Are there problems with the physical condition
    of the building (outdated systems, inflexible floor
    plans, ADA problems, difficulty in installing
    technology)?

    Comments: _____

    _____

B. Institutional Planning Team

1. Has an institutional library planning team been formed?

    Comments: _____

    _____

2. Who are the members of the library planning team:

    a) A representative of the legal owner (university,
        city, etc.)?

    b) Library representatives?

    c) Users (faculty, students, citizens, etc.)?

    d) Other representatives with technical skills such as
        engineering, legal, financial, architectural,
        buildings, etc.?

    e) Others (Friends of the Library, library committee
        members, etc.)?

    Comments: _____

    _____

3. What roles will members of the library planning play:

    a) Advising (gathering and disseminating information
        about the project)?

    b) Innovating (suggesting new ideas or new ways
        of tackling old problems)?

	YES	NO	N/A

c) Promoting ("selling" the project to interested stakeholders)? ___ ___ ___

d) Developing (assessing and developing ideas for practical implementation)? ___ ___ ___

e) Maintaining (ensuring that the infrastructure is in place so that the team can work with maximum efficiency)? ___ ___ ___

f) Linking (coordinating all work roles to ensure maximum cooperation and interchange of ideas, expertise, and experience)? ___ ___ ___

Comments: _____

_____

4. Who will be the spokesperson and chief contact for the institution on the project? ___ ___ ___

Comments: _____

_____

5. How will conflict be resolved on the project? ___ ___ ___

Comments: _____

_____

C. Determining Space Needs

1. Has a building program been prepared detailing space needs, adjacencies, and unique functions and features of the proposed building? ___ ___ ___

Comments: _____

_____

2. Has the library-building consultant prepared the program or advised staff on preparing the program? ___ ___ ___

Comments: _____

_____

3. Have the Association of College and Research Libraries *Standards for University Libraries: Evaluation of Performance,* Standards been consulted? ___ ___ ___

Comments: _____

_____

4. Have the Association of College and Research Libraries *Standards for College Libraries,* 2000 edition, Facilities questions been consulted? ___ ___ ___

	YES	NO	N/A

Comments: _____
_____

5. Has *Planning for Results: A Public Library Transformation Process* been consulted?   ____ ____ ____
   Comments: _____
   _____

6. Has the 1962 *Interim Standards for Small Public Libraries* been consulted? (This standard has never been rescinded and is the only standard that recommends quantitative measures for public library size.)   ____ ____ ____
   Comments: _____
   _____

7. Has ALA's *Information Power: Guidelines for School Library Media Programs,* appendix C, "Library Media Facilities Guidelines," been consulted? (Provides quantitative recommendations.)   ____ ____ ____
   Comments: _____
   _____

8. Has LAMA's *Building Blocks for Library Space* been consulted? ____ ____ ____
   Comments: _____
   _____

9. How large are the libraries of similarly sized and structured institutions?   ____ ____ ____
   Comments: _____
   _____

10. What is the useful life of the new building? If it is an interim solution, how will this impact future needs?   ____ ____ ____
    Comments: _____
    _____

11. What existing programs will be discontinued in the new building?   ____ ____ ____
    Comments: _____
    _____

12. What new programs will be added in the new building? ____ ____ ____
    Comments: _____
    _____

13. What will be the growth of the collection over the next twenty years?   ____ ____ ____
    Comments: _____

	YES	NO	N/A

14. What will be the growth of seating requirements
over the next twenty years? ___ ___ ___
Comments: _____
_____

15. What technology will be required to support library
programs over the next twenty years? ___ ___ ___
Comments: _____
_____

16. What will be the growth of staff over the next
twenty years? ___ ___ ___
Comments: _____
_____

17. What can the library afford? ___ ___ ___
Comments: _____
_____

D. Joint Use Considerations

1. Is there another library that may offer potential
synergy for a joint use facility? ___ ___ ___
Comments: _____
_____

2. Do the missions of the libraries considering a joint
facility have enough commonalities to enhance the
chances of success? ___ ___ ___
Comments: _____
_____

3. Are there possible efficiency and cost savings by
having a joint facility? ___ ___ ___
Comments: _____
_____

4. Can the quality and quantity of service be improved
for both libraries through a joint facility? ___ ___ ___
Comments: _____
_____

5. If a joint facility is agreed to, has a joint interagency
agreement been negotiated? ___ ___ ___
Comments: _____
_____

	YES	NO	N/A

E. Alternatives to New Construction

1. Has the collection been weeded to eliminate unneeded books and media that take up space in the library?   ____ ____ ____

   Comments: _____

   _____

2. Has the library's programming been reviewed, and programs eliminated that are no longer required that take up space in the library?   ____ ____ ____

   Comments: _____

   _____

3. Is it possible to renovate and refurbish existing spaces (improve the quality of the spaces and the ability of their occupants to work within them productively) in order to update spaces for electronics, better customer service, and atmosphere?   ____ ____ ____

   Comments: _____

   _____

4. Is it possible to install high-density stacks to provide more book storage within the exact same book stack floor space area?   ____ ____ ____

   Comments: _____

   _____

5. Has the library investigated a storage facility for low-use books and journals, and other little used media and archival materials?   ____ ____ ____

   Comments: _____

   _____

6. Has the library investigated leased space for public and nonpublic sections and activities that could function effectively outside the library in another location?   ____ ____ ____

   Comments: _____

   _____

7. Has the library investigated adjacent buildings that might be acquired in order to add square footage to the existing library?   ____ ____ ____

   Comments: _____

   _____

	YES	NO	N/A

8. Has the library investigated modular buildings and/ or kiosks that might be acquired instead of new construction?

    Comments: _____

_____

F. Selecting a Library Building Consultant

1. Is there someone on the staff who has the necessary planning knowledge and experience of the functional needs and requirements of library buildings? (If not, a library building consultant should be retained.)

    Comments: _____

_____

2. Has the consultant been retained at the very start of the building planning process so that he or she can take part in every step of the project?

    Comments: _____

_____

3. Is the consultant listed in LAMA's *Library Buildings Consultant List*?

    Comments: _____

_____

4. Does the consultant have broad and diversified experience in planning new buildings, renovations and additions, and conversion of other buildings into library buildings?

    Comments: _____

_____

5. Does the consultant have the personal characteristics, experience, and skills necessary to assist a library in its unique planning and building needs?

    Comments: _____

_____

6. Does the consultant have the written and verbal communication skills required to interact with all stakeholders?

    Comments: _____

_____

	YES	NO	N/A

7. Does the consultant have the political skills necessary to listen and respond to the concerns of all who may have a stake in the building project?

   Comments: _____

   _____

8. Does the building consultant have the ability to explain a point of view and to persuade others of the importance of carrying out the consultant's recommendations?

   Comments: _____

   _____

9. Does the consultant have the organizational and record-keeping skills needed to document and respond to key events and activities during the project?

   Comments: _____

   _____

10. Will the consultant provide advice on the selection of the architect and other members of the building's technical planning team?

    Comments: _____

    _____

11. Is the consultant's schedule flexible enough for him or her to be available for meetings with the library's planning committee when required?

    Comments: _____

    _____

12. Is the consultant available by telephone, surface mail, or electronic communication to answer questions and provide guidance when his or her physical presence is not required?

    Comments: _____

    _____

G. Choosing an Architect

1. Does the library director play a major role in selection of the architect?

   Comments: _____

   _____

	YES	NO	N/A

2. Has the group responsible for selection of the architect developed selection criteria?

   Comments: _____

   _____

3. Does the architectural selection process include:

   a) Announcement of the proposed project in an official publication used by the client organization or in the general press?

   b) Submittals by interested firms?

   c) Provision of standardized forms so that a uniform evaluation of firms may be used during the evaluation process?

   d) Evaluation based on the selection criteria developed by the group responsible for selection of the architect?

   e) Interviews with the "short list" of firms that the selection group has decided best meets the selection criteria?

   f) Ranking of the top firms to identify the best-qualified firms?

   g) Selection of the top-ranked firm based on the interview discussions and the selection criteria?

   h) Notification of unsuccessful firms, and a debriefing as to why they were not selected?

   Comments: _____

   _____

4. While not necessarily recommended, does the selection process involve:

   a) Limited or open architectural competitions?

   b) Design/build competitions?

   c) Bidding among various competitors?

   Comments: _____

   _____

5. Is the architectural firm an individual, partnership, corporation, or joint venture?

   Comments: _____

   _____

	YES	NO	N/A

6. Who are the principals of the firm? ___ ___ ___
   Comments: _____
   _____

7. Who is the person who will be in charge of designing
   the project? ___ ___ ___
   Comments: _____
   _____

8. Who is the person who will supervise the project from
   design to completion? ___ ___ ___
   Comments: _____
   _____

9. Is the architect or architectural firm registered to
   practice in the state? ___ ___ ___
   Comments: _____
   _____

10. Is the architect of record registered to practice in the state? ___ ___ ___
    Comments: _____
    _____

11. Are all key personnel and subconsultants involved in the
    project from the architect's office identified? ___ ___ ___
    Comments: _____
    _____

12. Are the architect's support team members identified:
    the landscape architect, civil engineer, structural
    engineer, sanitary engineer, mechanical engineer,
    electrical engineer, ADA compliance officer, and any
    other key specialists involved in the project? ___ ___ ___
    Comments: _____
    _____

13. Are all members of the architect's support team
    part of the firm, or does the architect retain them
    as subconsultants? ___ ___ ___
    Comments: _____
    _____

14. Do the architect's workload and organization pro-
    vide enough resources to devote time and energy
    to the project? ___ ___ ___
    Comments: _____
    _____

	YES	NO	N/A

15. Does the architect have experience in working with public agencies?

    Comments: _____

_____

16. Does the architect have prior experience in designing libraries?

    Comments: _____

_____

17. If the architect has not worked with libraries, does the architect have a plan to become knowledgeable about library needs?

    Comments: _____

_____

18. Is the architect an empathetic listener, willing to understand library needs?

    Comments: _____

_____

19. How will the architect gather information about library operations, project site, and so forth?

    Comments: _____

_____

20. What is the architect's design philosophy?

    Comments: _____

_____

21. Will the architect place library needs before design considerations?

    Comments: _____

_____

22. Does the architect's workload allow the firm to devote adequate time to the project?

    Comments: _____

_____

23. Does the architect have solid reference reports from past clients?

    *Comments:*_____

_____

24. In projects completed by the architect:

    a) Did the projects come in at or under budget?

	YES	NO	N/A

b) Did the projects come in on time? ___ ___ ___

c) What is the extent of change orders in number and dollars? ___ ___ ___

d) If there have been change orders, has it been determined whose fault they were? (Not all change orders are the architect's fault.) ___ ___ ___

e) What litigation has occurred against the architect? ___ ___ ___

f) What litigation has occurred against the architect's former clients by the architect? ___ ___ ___

Comments: _____

_____

25. Does the architect have written and verbal communication skills required for interacting with all stakeholders? ___ ___ ___

Comments: _____

_____

26. Does the architect have the political skills necessary to listen and respond to the concerns of all external and internal building-project stakeholders? ___ ___ ___

Comments: _____

_____

27. Does the architect have the ability to explain the reasons for a point of view and to persuade others of the importance of carrying out his or her recommendations? ___ ___ ___

Comments: _____

_____

28. Is the architect's proposed fee within the library's budget? ___ ___ ___

Comments: _____

_____

H. Choosing a Contractor

1. Will the award of the construction contract be made by a competitive bidding process? ___ ___ ___

	YES	NO	N/A

*Comments:*_____

2. Is a call or invitation to bid advertised in an official
    publication used by the client organization or in the
    general press?

    Comments: _____

3. For purposes of soliciting bids and awarding a con-
    tract, has the library declared who the "owner" is?
    (Usually the owner has legal and financial jurisdiction
    over the operations of the library.)

    Comments: _____

4. Does the bidding period extend for a period of four
    to six weeks so that potential bidders may prepare
    their bids?

    Comments: _____

5. Are standardized bid forms provided so that a uniform
    evaluation of contractors may be used during the bid
    evaluation process?

    Comments: _____

6. Are the architect and a library representative available
    to answer technical questions from potential bidders
    during the bid period?

    Comments: _____

7. Have a time and place been specified for opening bids?

    Comments: _____

8. During the bid opening, are all bids made public?

    Comments: _____

9. After bids are received, are they "taken under advise-
    ment" by the owner so that the bids may be analyzed?

    Comments: _____

	YES	NO	N/A

10. During the bid analysis period, and before the contract is awarded, is the lowest bidder checked for responsibility and:

   a) Is the bid submitted complete, accurate, and in compliance with the requirements, drawings, and specifications provided by the owner? ____ ____ ____

   b) Does the contractor have sufficient staff to execute the scope of the project? ____ ____ ____

   c) Has the contractor been in business long enough to establish a "track record"? ____ ____ ____

   d) What references does the contractor provide? ____ ____ ____

   e) What is the contractor's record in successfully completing other projects? ____ ____ ____

   f) Does the contractor usually complete projects in the period specified? ____ ____ ____

   g) What litigation has occurred against the contractor? ____ ____ ____

   h) What litigation has the contractor brought against previous clients and/or architects? ____ ____ ____

   i) What is the reputation of the subcontractors that the contractor has specified? ____ ____ ____

   j) Does the contractor have the necessary insurance and bonds to protect the owner as called for in the legal and financial specifications? ____ ____ ____

   k) Does the contractor have the appropriate licenses to do the job? ____ ____ ____

   Comments: _____

   _____

11. Is the bid awarded to the lowest responsible bidder? ____ ____ ____
   Comments: _____

   _____

I. Architectural Design

1. Does the library design meet the program requirements? ____ ____ ____
   Comments: _____

   _____

	YES	NO	N/A

2. Does the design have the character and power to make the library building a focus for its community or campus?

   Comments: _____

3. Does the design take full advantage of all positive features of the site?

   Comments: _____

4. Does the design compensate to the best degree possible for the negative aspects of the site?

   Comments: _____

5. Is the architectural character distinctive in appearance, yet in harmony with its surroundings?

   Comments: _____

6. Does the design welcome users and encourage nonusers?

   Comments: _____

7. Does the design create a building that is unmistakably public in character and function, yet very comfortable and nonintimidating for the user?

   Comments: _____

8. Is the interior design in harmony with the exterior of the library?

   Comments: _____

9. Do interior finishes create a space that is inviting to users, yet able to stand up to the wear and tear of heavy public use?

   Comments: _____

10. Does the design provide the flexibility to take advantage of changes in library products and services as well as technology?

   Comments: _____

	YES	NO	N/A

11. Does the design consider light, books, people, and the surrounding space as integral to each other? ____ ____ ____
    Comments: _____
    _____

12. Does the design express symbolically the important values of knowledge and learning? ____ ____ ____
    Comments: _____
    _____

13. Does the design merchandise the products and services of the library by incorporating design features used successfully in retail merchandising? ____ ____ ____
    Comments: _____
    _____

14. Does the design solve the paradoxical needs within a library of spatial openness and seclusion by creating:

    a) The ability to orient oneself within the visible total enclosure yet feel anchored to a particular part of it? ____ ____ ____

    b) The possibility of easy supervision by staff without the sense of being left exposed in a large impersonal space? ____ ____ ____

    c) A gradation of different spaces within the library, ranging from open areas of public activity to alcoves of semiprivate activity? ____ ____ ____

    d) Areas that have a sense of intimacy within the overall public setting? ____ ____ ____

    e) A wide variety of reading areas so that users have many choices to fit their mood or reading environment needs? ____ ____ ____

    f) A clear understanding upon entry to the library (and while moving within the library) of the general purpose of each library area? ____ ____ ____

    g) Clearly visible staff areas as a means for bringing information, services, and people together? ____ ____ ____

    Comments: _____
    _____

15. Does the library design plan encourage efficient traffic patterns from outside the structure into the building? ____ ____ ____
    Comments: _____
    _____

	YES	NO	N/A

16. Does the library design plan encourage efficient traffic patterns within the building?

Comments: _____

_____

17. Does the library design provide for the maximum use of self-service by the library's customers?

Comments: _____

_____

18. Does the design reflect the unique natural climate of the region where it is located?

Comments: _____

_____

19. Are windows treated or shaded to prevent the hot and damaging rays of the sun from penetrating the interiors?

Comments: _____

_____

20. Does the design provide flexibility in the placement of lighting fixtures, air ducts and registers, electrical power, and communication linkages to provide long-term flexibility?

Comments: _____

_____

21. Does the spacing of columns, shafts, and other architectural elements provide flexibility and the effective use of space?

Comments: _____

_____

22. Does the modular system employed meet the unique space needs of the library?

Comments: _____

_____

J. Sustainable Design

1. Is the new building or renovation designed and constructed in ways that preserve the natural outdoor environment and promote a healthful indoor habitat?

Comments: _____

_____

	YES	NO	N/A

2. Is the building project designed to avoid inflicting permanent adverse impact on the natural state of the air, land, and water, by using resources and methods that minimize pollution and waste, and do not cause permanent damage to the earth, including erosion?   ____   ____   ____
   Comments: _____

3. Is the building designed to take the maximum advantage of passive and natural sources of heat, cooling, ventilation, and light?   ____   ____   ____
   Comments: _____

4. Are innovative strategies and technologies such as porous paving to conserve water, reduce effluent and run-off, thus recharging the water table employed?   ____   ____   ____
   Comments: _____

5. Is the project planned to reduce the need for individual automobiles, use alternative fuels, and encourage public and alternate modes of transportation such as bicycling and public transportation?   ____   ____   ____
   Comments: _____

6. Is the building constructed and operated using materials, methods, mechanical and electrical systems that ensure a healthful indoor air quality, while avoiding contamination by carcinogens, volatile organic compounds, fungi, molds, bacteria, and other known toxins?   ____   ____   ____
   Comments: _____

7. Are the HVAC system's outdoor air intakes located as high as possible above the ground and far enough away from the exhaust ducts to reduce the intake of ground level air pollution (exhaust from traffic)?   ____   ____   ____
   Comments: _____

8. Are stainless-steel-strip bird guards installed over the horizontal rooftop outdoor air intakes to prevent birds from settling on the grating and polluting the shafts below?   ____   ____   ____
   Comments: _____

	YES	NO	N/A

9. Does the HVAC have an efficiency air filtration system with pre-filters and final filters at 30 percent and 85 percent efficiency respectively? ____ ____ ____

    Comments: _____

10. Are air filters designed to be easy to access and clean and/or replace? ____ ____ ____

    Comments: _____

11. Has the exposed fiberglass (porous insulation) within the HVAC system been encapsulated to eliminate amplification sites for fungal and bacterial micro-organisms? ____ ____ ____

    Comments: _____

12. Is the rate of ventilation with outdoor air at the rate of 25 cubic feet per minute? ____ ____ ____

    Comments: _____

13. Are copy rooms and similar spaces that emit possibly toxic substances equipped with their own dedicated air exhaust systems? ____ ____ ____

    Comments: _____

14. Are particleboards that emit formaldehyde emissions prohibited in the building? ____ ____ ____

    Comments: _____

15. Are only solvent-free paints specified for the project? ____ ____ ____

    Comments: _____

16. Are low-emitting, solvent-free adhesives specified for the project? ____ ____ ____

    Comments: _____

17. Is furniture constructed without particle boards that emit formaldehyde? ____ ____ ____

    Comments: _____

Library Site Selection

	YES	NO	N/A

A. General Conditions

1. Is the site conveniently located to the population served by the library? ___ ___ ___

   Comments: _____

   _____

2. Does the site provide high visibility and identification to the population served? ___ ___ ___

   Comments: _____

   _____

3. Is the site affordable? ___ ___ ___

   Comments: _____

   _____

4. Will the site provide visibility of the building and its function from the street? ___ ___ ___

   Comments: _____

   _____

5. Will a library be an appropriate use of the land parcel in question? ___ ___ ___

   Comments: _____

   _____

		YES	NO	N/A

6. Will the site retain or enhance the natural contours of the land?

    Comments: _____

_____

7. Is the site zoned for a library? If not, is future library zoning possible?

    Comments: _____

_____

8. Are there existing structures on the site that must be demolished?

    Comments: _____

_____

9. If an existing structure must be demolished, does it present asbestos, lead paint, or unusual environmental problems?

    Comments: _____

_____

10. If the library is to be a branch of a system, are there overlapping service areas from other branches in the system?

    Comments: _____

_____

11. Will the use of the site for a library add aesthetic value or other amenities to the neighborhood?

    Comments: _____

_____

12. Are there liabilities or nuisance factors to adjacent properties and their activities?

    Comments: _____

_____

13. Will the use of the site for a library have any negative impact on the surrounding areas?

    Comments: _____

_____

14. Will the library fit in with the architectural style of neighboring buildings?

    Comments: _____

_____

	YES	NO	N/A

15. Will the building work with the traffic flow of adjacent areas? ____ ____ ____

   Comments: _____

   _____

B. Location

1. Is the location of the site considered satisfactory and acceptable by the population being served? ____ ____ ____

   Comments: _____

   _____

2. Is the site accessible to all segments of the community being served? ____ ____ ____

   Comments: _____

   _____

3. Is the site relatively close to the part of the community that is understood to be most active, and that will generate the most use? ____ ____ ____

   Comments: _____

   _____

4. Is the site appropriate for the library given its function and clientele? ____ ____ ____

   Comments: _____

   _____

5. Would library usage

   a) Increase if another site was selected? ____ ____ ____

   b) Decrease if another site was selected? ____ ____ ____

   c) Stay the same if another site was selected? ____ ____ ____

   Comments: _____

   _____

6. Will this location best meet the library objective of providing materials and services to the greatest number of people at the lowest cost? ____ ____ ____

   Comments: _____

   _____

	YES	NO	N/A
7. Is the location in an area that is frequently visited by members of the community for daily activities such as shopping, working, and seeking out other services?	____	____	____
Comments: _____			
8. Is the site located near commercial, retail, cultural, and other activities within the community?	____	____	____
Comments: _____			
9. Does the proposed site present a safety issue for patrons and library staff?	____	____	____
Comments: _____			

C. Accessibility

	YES	NO	N/A
1. Is the site easily accessible to those living in the area served?	____	____	____
Comments: _____			
2. Is the site easily reached by the greatest number of potential customers?	____	____	____
Comments: _____			
3. Are travel times from target population areas to the library acceptable?	____	____	____
Comments: _____			
4. Have automobile traffic patterns near the library been considered?	____	____	____
Comments: _____			
5. Is the site located on a busy highway that will require a separate street-type entrance or driveway?	____	____	____
Comments: _____			

	YES	NO	N/A

6. Is the site accessible to public transportation? ____ ____ ____
   Comments: _____

   _____

7. Is bicycle access encouraged? ____ ____ ____
   Comments: _____

   _____

8. Are there sidewalks for pedestrian access? ____ ____ ____
   Comments: _____

   _____

9. Is the site conveniently accessible to private vehicle
   transportation? ____ ____ ____
   Comments: _____

   _____

10. Does the entrance to the library provide adequate
    space and ease of accessibility to accommodate all
    arriving individuals and groups at all times? ____ ____ ____
    Comments: _____

    _____

D. Size

1. Does the size of the site provide adequate space for
   current needs? ____ ____ ____
   Comments: _____

   _____

2. Will the site provide room for future expansion
   and/or remodeling? ____ ____ ____
   Comments: _____

   _____

3. Does the site include enough space for
   appropriate green space and landscaping? ____ ____ ____
   Comments: _____

   _____

4. Is the site large enough to accommodate on-site
   parking? ____ ____ ____
   Comments: _____

   _____

	YES	NO	N/A

5. Does the property contain possible easements? ___ ___ ___

   Comments: _____

   _____

6. Does the property accommodate adequate setbacks
   to meet zoning and aesthetic considerations? ___ ___ ___

   Comments: _____

   _____

7. Is the property configuration adequate for successful
   completion of the building project? ___ ___ ___

   Comments: _____

   _____

8. Is there enough space on the property and/or adjacent
   to it for staging during construction? ___ ___ ___

   Comments: _____

   _____

E. Environmental Issues

1. Has an environmental impact report been made for
   the proposed site? ___ ___ ___

   Comments: _____

   _____

2. Is the site oriented so that it is possible to take
   advantage of solar energy? ___ ___ ___

   Comments: _____

   _____

3. Are complications likely to arise from the nature of
   the ground beneath the building? ___ ___ ___

   Comments: _____

   _____

4. Does the site have adequate drainage? ___ ___ ___

   Comments: _____

   _____

5. Is the site above the level of a 100-year flood plain? ___ ___ ___

   Comments: _____

   _____

	YES	NO	N/A

6. Has a subsurface probe been done to examine soil
   conditions, utilities, and other factors?   ___ ___ ___
   Comments: _____
   _____

7. Has the site been improved; that is, are curbs, gutters,
   water, sewers, and electricity available?   ___ ___ ___
   Comments: _____
   _____

8. Are there any natural or artificial barriers?   ___ ___ ___
   Comments: _____
   _____

9. Are there any hidden problems of geology, topog-
   raphy, archaeology, buried objects, or toxic waste?   ___ ___ ___
   Comments: _____
   _____

10. Do neighboring facilities pose possible environmental/
    nuisance problems?   ___ ___ ___
    Comments: _____
    _____

11. Has the condition of the soil been tested to determine
    the stability of the site?   ___ ___ ___
    Comments: _____
    _____

12. Are there advantages to the slope of the land?   ___ ___ ___
    Comments: _____
    _____

13. Are there disadvantages to the slope of the land?   ___ ___ ___
    Comments: _____
    _____

3

General Exterior Considerations

	YES	NO	N/A

A. Landscaping

1. Has the landscape design been considered early in the planning and design stage?   ____   ____   ____

   Comments: _____

   _____

2. Has a landscape architect been retained as one of the architect's subconsultants?   ____   ____   ____

   Comments: _____

   _____

3. Does the landscape design enhance the overall design of the building?   ____   ____   ____

   Comments: _____

   _____

4. Does the landscaping complement and enhance the site and adjoining neighborhood?   ____   ____   ____

   Comments: _____

   _____

5. Is the landscaping visually satisfying and inviting?   ____   ____   ____

   Comments: _____

   _____

	YES	NO	N/A

6. Is the landscaping design in harmony with the climatic
    zone of the library site?

    Comments: _____

    _____

7. Do the plants selected provide pleasing colors and
    textures throughout all seasons of the year?

    Comments: _____

    _____

8. Is the landscaping designed from both an interior
    and exterior perspective?

    Comments: _____

    _____

9. Is there an adequate amount of good soil?

    Comments: _____

    _____

10. Is there adequate drainage?

    Comments: _____

    _____

11. Are the plants selected appropriate to the amount of
    sun and/or shade they will receive?

    Comments: _____

    _____

12. Do trees and shrubs enhance the building's energy
    and water conservation efforts?

    Comments: _____

    _____

13. Are the plants and shrubs selected not subject to
    damaging attacks by insects or disease?

    Comments: _____

    _____

14. Can the landscaping be easily and inexpensively
    maintained?

    Comments: _____

    _____

15. Is there an automatic irrigation system in place?

    *Comments:*_____

    _____

	YES	NO	N/A

16. Is the parking area landscaped in conformance with local codes and regulations? ___ ___ ___
    Comments: _____

17. Is a local garden club or community organization willing to provide volunteer gardening as a public service? ___ ___ ___
    Comments: _____

B. Parking

1. Are there sufficient parking spaces for staff as well as customers during all service hours? ___ ___ ___
   Comments: _____

2. Does the site provide adequate parking spaces to meet institutional and local parking codes? ___ ___ ___
   Comments: _____

3. Do handicapped parking spaces meet or exceed ADA regulations in both number and specifications? ___ ___ ___
   Comments: _____

4. Is parking convenient to the library's entrances? ___ ___ ___
   Comments: _____

5. Is the parking area well lighted at night? ___ ___ ___
   Comments: _____

6. Is there adequate parking for large cars and trucks? ___ ___ ___
   Comments: _____

7. If there is a parking garage, is it close to the library's public entrance? ___ ___ ___
   Comments: _____

	YES	NO	N/A

8. Is the parking garage well identified from the street? _____ _____ _____
   Comments: _____

   _____

9. Is the parking garage secure and well lighted at all times? _____ _____ _____
   Comments: _____

   _____

10. Can cars easily get in and out of parking lots and/or
    structures? _____ _____ _____
    Comments: _____

    _____

11. If the library has an employee recognition program,
    is there a designated parking space for "employee of
    the month" very near the staff or receiving entrance? _____ _____ _____
    Comments: _____

    _____

12. If there is a bookmobile, is parking convenient for staff
    to move materials on and off the vehicle? _____ _____ _____
    Comments: _____

    _____

13. If there is a community room, is there adequate parking
    for the number of extra cars that will need to be parked? _____ _____ _____
    Comments: _____

    _____

14. In northern climates, is there adequate room for snow-
    plow access as well as snow stacking space? _____ _____ _____
    Comments: _____

    _____

15. Does the institution subsidize parking if free parking
    is not available? _____ _____ _____
    Comments: _____

    _____

16. If the library parking is metered, does the library
    provide convenient coin-changing machines? _____ _____ _____
    Comments: _____

    _____

17. If the library does not provide parking, is public
    parking available nearby? _____ _____ _____
    Comments: _____

    _____

	YES	NO	N/A

C. Building Exterior

1. Is the building aesthetically pleasing during the day
   and night?   ___ ___ ___
   Comments: _____

   _____

2. Is the fenestration arranged to take maximum advantage of natural light and the best views, while allowing
   use of floor and wall space inside the building?   ___ ___ ___
   Comments: _____

   _____

3. Will sunlight, glare, and excessive ultraviolet rays be
   controlled architecturally?   ___ ___ ___
   Comments: _____

   _____

4. Are all exterior architectural features and surfaces
   constructed of easily maintained materials?   ___ ___ ___
   Comments: _____

   _____

5. Do walls have a hard texture that is not easily
   scratched?   ___ ___ ___
   Comments: _____

   _____

6. Do walls have a graffiti-repellent coating?   ___ ___ ___
   Comments: _____

   _____

7. Do all exterior access walks and surfaces meet ADA
   requirements?   ___ ___ ___
   Comments: _____

   _____

8. Are all walkways and ramps leading into the building well lighted?   ___ ___ ___
   Comments: _____

   _____

9. In northern areas, do sidewalk lamps give off heat
   to help melt snow and ice?   ___ ___ ___
   Comments: _____

   _____

	YES	NO	N/A

10. Are walkway surfaces stable and firm? ___ ___ ___
Comments: _____
_____

11. Are walkway surfaces slip-resistant? ___ ___ ___
Comments: _____
_____

12. Are stair steps uniform in height and width? ___ ___ ___
Comments: _____
_____

13. Is there a separate staff entrance? ___ ___ ___
Comments: _____
_____

14. Are public telephones available outside? ___ ___ ___
Comments: _____
_____

15. Is there provision for storage of lawn mowers, snowblowers, and other outside equipment? ___ ___ ___
Comments: _____
_____

16. Is there provision outside for vandal-proof faucets
and electrical outlets? ___ ___ ___
Comments: _____
_____

D. Roof

1. In northern areas, is the roof peaked? ___ ___ ___
Comments: _____
_____

2. Are drainage systems on the roof adequate to carry
off water from heavy downpours or melted snow? ___ ___ ___
Comments: _____
_____

3. Are the roof and eaves area well insulated to allow
for maximum energy efficiency? ___ ___ ___
Comments: _____

	YES	NO	N/A

4. Is the building's roof easily maintained? ___ ___ ___
    Comments: _____

    _____

5. Are entrances and walkways protected from avalanches
    of water, snow, or ice accumulated on the roof? ___ ___ ___
    Comments: _____

    _____

6. Do downspouts carry the water away from the build-
    ing and sidewalks into storm drains? ___ ___ ___
    Comments: _____

    _____

E. Bicycle Racks

1. Are bicycle racks clearly visible from the street and/
    or interior? ___ ___ ___
    Comments: _____

    _____

2. Are bicycle racks convenient to the building entrances? ___ ___ ___
    Comments: _____

    _____

3. Are bicycle racks equipped with locks? ___ ___ ___
    Comments: _____

    _____

4. Are the bicycle racks in a well-lighted area? ___ ___ ___
    Comments: _____

    _____

F. Flagpole

1. Is there a flagpole outside the building? ___ ___ ___
    Comments: _____

    _____

2. Is it a ground-set, wall-mounted, or roof-mounted pole? ___ ___ ___
    Comments: _____

    _____

	YES	NO	N/A

3. Is there a self-storing flagpole shaft? ____ ____ ____

Comments: _____

_____

4. Can the flag be raised, lowered, and drawn into the pole either manually or electrically? ____ ____ ____

Comments: _____

_____

5. Is it safe from vandalism? ____ ____ ____

Comments: _____

_____

6. If the flag is to be flown at night, is it adequately lighted? ____ ____ ____

Comments: _____

_____

G. Exterior Signage

1. Is signage incorporated into the preliminary design of the site, parking, and building? ____ ____ ____

Comments: _____

_____

2. Does signage comply with ADAAG (ADA Accessibility Guidelines for Buildings and Facilities)? ____ ____ ____

Comments: _____

_____

3. Is the standard international symbol for libraries displayed? ____ ____ ____

Comments: _____

_____

4. Is there a large, exterior, well-lit sign identifying the library? ____ ____ ____

Comments: _____

_____

5. Is the exterior sign clearly visible from passing cars during the day and night? ____ ____ ____

Comments: _____

_____

	YES	NO	N/A

6. Does the sign have space for advertising of library events, holiday hours, etc.? _____ _____ _____

   Comments: _____

   _____

7. Are the library's hours of service prominently displayed on a large, well-lit sign at the entrance along with an OPEN/CLOSED sign? _____ _____ _____

   Comments: _____

   _____

8. Do the colors of the letters contrast with the color of the sign and complement the outside of the building? _____ _____ _____

   Comments: _____

   _____

9. Are signs attached to the wall adjacent to the latch side of the door? _____ _____ _____

   Comments: _____

   _____

10. Would a map, directory, or graphic be more appropriate than a sign? _____ _____ _____

    Comments: _____

    _____

11. Do pictorial signs have verbal descriptions placed below the picture? _____ _____ _____

    Comments: _____

    _____

12. Are the letters in sans serif or simple serif? _____ _____ _____

    Comments: _____

    _____

13. Do signs have a nonglare finish? _____ _____ _____

    Comments: _____

    _____

14. When selecting sign size, have background and distance been considered? _____ _____ _____

    Comments: _____

    _____

15. Is sign size 1 inch for every 50 feet of visibility and a minimum of 3 inches? _____ _____ _____

    Comments: _____

    _____

	YES	NO	N/A

16. Has negative phrasing been avoided in signage? ____ ____ ____
   Comments: _____
   _____

17. Are the signs durable and can they be easily and
   cost-effectively replaced? ____ ____ ____
   Comments: _____
   _____

18. Are signs read horizontally and not vertically? ____ ____ ____
   Comments: _____
   _____

19. If there is an arrow to indicate direction, is it separate
   from the lettered sign so that it can be changed if
   necessary? ____ ____ ____
   Comments: _____
   _____

H. Delivery

1. Is there a sheltered entrance or loading dock for
   deliveries from all types of vehicles? ____ ____ ____
   Comments: _____
   _____

2. If there is no loading dock, is parking for delivery
   vehicles located close to the exit nearest the
   delivery or workroom? ____ ____ ____
   Comments: _____
   _____

3. Is the delivery area a separate room? ____ ____ ____
   Comments: _____
   _____

4. Are there two separate counters/tables in the delivery
   area so that delivery staff can distinguish between
   outgoing and incoming packages? ____ ____ ____
   Comments: _____
   _____

	YES	NO	N/A

5. Do the counters/tables have enough length and breadth to provide sufficient space for peak loading times? ____ ____ ____

Comments: _____

_____

6. Are the counters/tables a comfortable height so as to avoid physical injury from lifting? ____ ____ ____

Comments: _____

_____

7. Is the delivery area clearly marked and easily accessible from the street? ____ ____ ____

Comments:_____

_____

8. Is there a buzzer and/or internal telephone at or near the delivery entrance? ____ ____ ____

Comments: _____

_____

9. Does the loading dock have a device that will accommodate trucks with beds of different heights? (Docks with a height of 48 inches will accommodate most delivery trucks, but not vans for which a lower height is preferred.) ____ ____ ____

Comments: _____

_____

10. Does the loading dock have a minimum overhead clearance of 14 feet? ____ ____ ____

Comments: _____

_____

11. Is the loading dock located away from the primary work and public areas so that noise and fumes do not disturb staff or users? ____ ____ ____

Comments: _____

_____

12. Are building exhaust fumes addressed in the design? ____ ____ ____

Comments: _____

_____

13. Can delivery trucks be easily unloaded? ____ ____ ____

Comments: _____

_____

	YES	NO	N/A

14. Is there generous space for easy truck turnaround? ____ ____ ____
Comments: _____
_____

15. Is there provision for the temporary storage and
pickup of trash? ____ ____ ____
Comments: _____
_____

16. Is the trash area secure from "dumpster divers"? ____ ____ ____
Comments: _____
_____

I. Book Returns

1. Is there an after-hours book return? ____ ____ ____
Comments: _____
_____

2. Does the book return meet ADA requirements? ____ ____ ____
Comments: _____
_____

3. Is the book-return area well lighted and secure? ____ ____ ____
Comments: _____
_____

4. Is the book return sheltered from the weather and
small creatures? ____ ____ ____
Comments: _____
_____

5. Is the book return part of the building and accessible
from the inside rather than separate from the building? ____ ____ ____
Comments: _____
_____

6. Is the book return fire-retardant? ____ ____ ____
Comments: _____
_____

7. Does the book-return area have a smoke detector? ____ ____ ____
Comments: _____
_____

	YES	NO	N/A
8. Is the book return visible to patrons in automobiles? *Comments:* _____	___	___	___
9. Is the book return accessible from an automobile? *Comments:* _____	___	___	___
10. Is the book return designed so that it will not damage books as it is used? *Comments:* _____	___	___	___
11. Does the door on the book return lock when the cart is full to prevent cart overflowing? *Comments:* _____	___	___	___
12. Is there a separate return for audiovisual materials? *Comments:* _____	___	___	___
13. Is there a locking device on outside book returns? *Comments:* _____	___	___	___
14. Do outside book returns accommodate both walk-up and drive-up access through two deposit openings? *Comments:* _____	___	___	___

Interior Organization of Library Buildings

	YES	NO	N/A

A. Entrance

1. For security purposes, is there only one public entrance/exit?

   Comments: _____

2. Is the staff entrance secured from unauthorized use and well lighted?

   Comments: _____

3. Is the building's entrance easily identifiable to pedestrians as well as people in cars?

   Comments: _____

4. Is the route from the public transportation stop to the entrance easily accessible?

   Comments: _____

5. Are all building entrances sheltered from the weather and well lighted?

   Comments: _____

	YES	NO	N/A

6. Is a floor covering or system provided near the entrance that allows for removal of debris from users' shoes as they walk into a building?   ____ ____ ____

   Comments: _____

_____

7. Is there a floor drain provided for exterior rain and snow removal at the entrance to the building?   ____ ____ ____

   Comments: _____

_____

8. Are there trash and cigarette receptacles near each of the entrances?   ____ ____ ____

   Comments: _____

_____

9. Are the outside telephones well lighted at night and easily visible?   ____ ____ ____

   Comments: _____

_____

10. Is there outside seating available?   ____ ____ ____

   Comments: _____

_____

11. If the library is at an intersection, is there a main entrance at or near a corner that will serve both streets?   ____ ____ ____

   Comments: _____

_____

12. Is there a double-door vestibule to prevent drafts and heat and/or air conditioning losses?   ____ ____ ____

   Comments: _____

_____

13. Is the hardware for the entrance doors durable and sturdy enough to withstand heavy use?   ____ ____ ____

   Comments: _____

_____

14. Are entrance doors easy to open and close?   ____ ____ ____

   Comments: _____

_____

15. Has safety glass been used in the entrance area?   ____ ____ ____

   Comments: _____

_____

	YES	NO	N/A

16. Are all public-service elements of the building easily located from the entrance? ___ ___ ___

   Comments: _____

   _____

17. Is there a book security system? ___ ___ ___

   Comments: _____

   _____

18. Can the book security system be installed without surface mounted wiring or carpet runners? ___ ___ ___

   Comments: _____

   _____

19. If a metal studding system is used in framing the building, are wood studs used adjacent to the area where the book security system is installed to prevent interference? ___ ___ ___

   Comments: _____

   _____

20. Are the various areas within the interior identified by signs, lighting, color, and furnishings? Do the areas listed below stand out when one enters the building:

   a) Circulation? ___ ___ ___

   b) Reference/information? ___ ___ ___

   c) Catalog? ___ ___ ___

   d) Books/audiovisual? ___ ___ ___

   e) Children/adults/young adults? ___ ___ ___

   Comments: _____

   _____

21. Are furniture and equipment used to promote, merchandise, and display some parts of the book and media collections of the library? ___ ___ ___

   Comments: _____

   _____

22. Is there space near the entrance for:

   a) Public bulletin boards? ___ ___ ___

   b) Display cases? ___ ___ ___

   c) Pamphlet racks? ___ ___ ___

   d) Announcements of library events? ___ ___ ___

	YES	NO	N/A
e) Community announcements bulletin boards?	___	___	___
f) Public telephones?	___	___	___
g) Vending machines?	___	___	___
h) Book donation drop?	___	___	___
i) Lobby seating?	___	___	___

Comments: _____

_____

23. Does there appear to be good traffic flow throughout the interior?   ___ ___ ___

Comments:_____

_____

B. Circulation Desk Facilities

1. Is the circulation area located near the library's entrance? ___ ___ ___

   Comments: _____

   _____

2. Is the circulation area clearly visible and identifiable from the library's entrance?   ___ ___ ___

   Comments: _____

   _____

3. Is there enough space between the circulation and security equipment to prevent one system from interfering with the electrical and physical operation of the other?   ___ ___ ___

   Comments: _____

   _____

4. Are the following functions easily identified and located by library users:

   a) Checkout?   ___ ___ ___

   b) Self or express checkout (if available)?   ___ ___ ___

   c) Returns?   ___ ___ ___

   d) Library cards?   ___ ___ ___

   e) Information/inquiry?   ___ ___ ___

   f) Reserve/holds?   ___ ___ ___

	YES	NO	N/A

g) Interlibrary loan? ___ ___ ___

h) Other? ___ ___ ___

Comments: _____

_____

5. Are queuing provisions made for a smooth traffic flow
    for entering and leaving the building without obstacles
    created by checkout lines during peak periods? ___ ___ ___

    Comments: _____

    _____

6. Will checkout lines be long enough to require stanchions
    and roping? ___ ___ ___

    Comments: _____

    _____

7. Does the circulation desk accommodate:

    a) Computer checkout terminals? ___ ___ ___

    b) Self-checkout terminals? ___ ___ ___

    c) Terminal screens that are visible to customers? ___ ___ ___

    d) Telephones? ___ ___ ___

    e) Answering machines? ___ ___ ___

    f) Cash registers and/or cash drawers? ___ ___ ___

    g) Lost and found items? ___ ___ ___

    Comments: _____

    _____

8. Are there sufficient sorting shelves and trucks for
    holding returned materials? ___ ___ ___

    Comments: _____

    _____

9. Are the shelves and trucks easily accessible and
    clearly arranged? ___ ___ ___

    Comments: _____

    _____

10. Can the shelves accommodate all sizes of returned
    materials? ___ ___ ___

    Comments: _____

    _____

	YES	NO	N/A

11. Is there an interior book drop and can it be easily cleared?

    Comments: _____

    _____

12. Is there adequate work space for staff?

    Comments: _____

    _____

13. Is there toe space and knee space incorporated into the counter for staff comfort and convenience?

    Comments: _____

    _____

14. Is the circulation desk the appropriate height for adults, children, and disabled customers?

    Comments: _____

    _____

15. Is the desk designed for a logical work flow based on the circulation system employed by the library?

    Comments: _____

    _____

16. Is there adequate space for book trucks to move about and through the circulation area?

    Comments: _____

    _____

17. Are sorting shelves and trucks easily accessible from the return portions of the desk?

    Comments: _____

    _____

18. Is the top of the desk covered with a material that does not get damaged when heavy materials and equipment are dragged across or dropped upon it?

    Comments: _____

    _____

19. Can the desk surface be cleaned easily on a daily basis?

    Comments: _____

    _____

20. Is the flooring material adjacent to the circulation counter of a type that will minimize noise of book trucks?

    Comments: _____

    _____

	YES	NO	N/A

21. Is there shock-absorbent flooring next to the staff side of the circulation desk?

    _____ _____ _____

    Comments: _____

    _____

22. Is the floor adjacent to the circulation counter easily maintained and safe during wet weather?

    _____ _____ _____

    Comments: _____

    _____

23. Are circulation staff offices located near the circulation area?

    _____ _____ _____

    Comments: _____

    _____

24. Is the circulation desk accessible to both children and disabled users?

    _____ _____ _____

    Comments: _____

    _____

25. Are the height and width of the circulation desk appropriate for the various work functions taking place?

    _____ _____ _____

    Comments: _____

    _____

26. Is the circulation desk modular in design so that modules may be interchanged as need arises?

    _____ _____ _____

    Comments: _____

    _____

27. Is the desk designed to handle the necessary equipment with hidden, yet accessible, wiring and cable?

    _____ _____ _____

    Comments: _____

    _____

28. Are the electrical wiring and cabling out of public view? _____ _____ _____

    Comments: _____

    _____

29. Are the electrical wiring and cabling easily accessible by staff?

    _____ _____ _____

    Comments: _____

    _____

30. Is the circulation desk designed to accommodate changing the location and size of electrical equipment in the future?

    _____ _____ _____

	YES	NO	N/A

Comments: _____

_____

31. Are keyboards ergonomically designed?   ____   ____   ____

Comments: _____

_____

32. Is the monitor screen visible to the customers?   ____   ____   ____

Comments: _____

_____

33. Are there back panels on the computers to screen
them from the public?   ____   ____   ____

Comments: _____

_____

34. If there is a materials security system, is there space
for the sensitizing and desensitizing equipment?   ____   ____   ____

Comments: _____

_____

35. Is there room to expand the desk as circulation
of materials increases?   ____   ____   ____

Comments: _____

_____

C. Reference Facilities

1. Is the reference desk clearly identified and conveniently located?   ____   ____   ____

Comments: _____

_____

2. Is the reference desk the appropriate height for adults,
children, and disabled patrons?   ____   ____   ____

Comments: _____

_____

3. Is the reference area arranged in such a manner that
librarians are visibly approachable?   ____   ____   ____

Comments: _____

_____

	YES	NO	N/A

4. Is the reference desk located where staff can identify by sight those customers having difficulty finding reference materials? ___ ___ ___

   Comments: _____

   _____

5. Is there seating for customer/staff consultation? ___ ___ ___

   Comments: _____

   _____

6. Can reference librarians easily get out from behind the desk to help customers? ___ ___ ___

   Comments: _____

   _____

7. Are reference collections, including ready reference materials, conveniently located and identified? ___ ___ ___

   Comments: _____

   _____

8. Are photocopiers close to the reference materials? ___ ___ ___

   Comments: _____

   _____

9. Are materials and equipment requiring staff assistance grouped close to the reference service desk? ___ ___ ___

   Comments: _____

   _____

10. Is there a terminal on the reference desk that can perform circulation functions as well as database searching functions? ___ ___ ___

    Comments: _____

    _____

11. Is the public access catalog accessible from all parts of the reference collection? ___ ___ ___

    Comments: _____

    _____

12. Are catalog terminals well distributed in the reference area? ___ ___ ___

    Comments: _____

    _____

13. Does the reference staff have adequate work space at their public service desk? ___ ___ ___

	YES	NO	N/A

Comments: _____

_____

14. Does the reference desk have a cordless phone in order to do more efficient interviews with telephone service customers while performing shelf checks?   ____   ____   ____

Comments: _____

_____

15. Does the telephone system have a multiline capacity?   ____   ____   ____

Comments: _____

_____

16. Are adequate space, appropriate lighting, and acoustics allowed for the following equipment and its use:

a) Computer terminals?   ____   ____   ____

b) CD-ROM units?   ____   ____   ____

c) Online-networking stations?   ____   ____   ____

d) Audiovisual equipment?   ____   ____   ____

e) Photocopiers?   ____   ____   ____

f) Microform equipment?   ____   ____   ____

g) Other?   ____   ____   ____

Comments: _____

_____

17. Is adequate space allowed for customer use of reference materials?   ____   ____   ____

Comments: _____

_____

18. Does the reference area provide separate or acoustically isolated spaces for the following services:

a) Interlibrary loan?   ____   ____   ____

b) Database searches?   ____   ____   ____

c) General information?   ____   ____   ____

d) Customer interviews?   ____   ____   ____

e) Telephone reference service?   ____   ____   ____

f) Photocopiers?   ____   ____   ____

Comments: _____

_____

	YES	NO	N/A

19. If the following materials are included in the reference collection, is adequate space allowed for their use, including the equipment they require:

a) Computer databases? ____ ____ ____

b) Newspapers? ____ ____ ____

c) Periodicals? ____ ____ ____

d) Indexes and abstracts? ____ ____ ____

e) Annual reports? ____ ____ ____

f) Bibliographies? ____ ____ ____

g) Unabridged dictionaries? ____ ____ ____

h) Microforms? ____ ____ ____

i) Rare books? ____ ____ ____

j) Government publications? ____ ____ ____

k) Vertical files? ____ ____ ____

l) Ready reference? ____ ____ ____

m) Reserves? ____ ____ ____

n) College catalogs and career information? ____ ____ ____

o) City directories? ____ ____ ____

p) Archives? ____ ____ ____

q) Telephone directories? ____ ____ ____

r) Genealogy resources? ____ ____ ____

s) Maps and atlases? ____ ____ ____

t) General reference materials? ____ ____ ____

u) Newspaper clippings? ____ ____ ____

v) Audiovisual materials? ____ ____ ____

w) Tax forms? ____ ____ ____

x) General information flyers? ____ ____ ____

y) Miscellaneous library and public information? ____ ____ ____

z) Other? ____ ____ ____

Comments: _____

		YES	NO	N/A
20.	Are there storage provisions for these materials?	___	___	___
	Comments: _____			
	_____			
21.	Are reference staff offices located near the reference area?	___	___	___
	Comments: _____			
	_____			
22.	If areas of limited or closed access exist, is adequate space allocated for:			
	a) Staffing?	___	___	___
	b) Expansion?	___	___	___
	c) Security?	___	___	___
	Comments: _____			
	_____			
23.	Does the reference staff have adequate work space at their public service desks?	___	___	___
	Comments: _____			
	_____			
24.	Can the public service areas be expanded for additional equipment?	___	___	___
	Comments: _____			
	_____			

D. Children's Facilities

		YES	NO	N/A
1.	Is the physical and psychological environment pleasant and inviting to children? If you were a child, would this area appeal to you?	___	___	___
	Comments: _____			
	_____			
2.	Is the children's area arranged in such a manner that adults are not reluctant to use it?	___	___	___
	Comments: _____			
	_____			
3.	If there is a children's staff office, is it of adequate size?	___	___	___
	Comments: _____			
	_____			

	YES	NO	N/A

4. Is there a separate children's card catalog or an online
   public access terminal? ___ ___ ___
   Comments: _____
   _____

5. Are shelving and furniture scaled for children? ___ ___ ___
   Comments: _____
   _____

6. Are there small alcoves, surrounded by low shelves,
   controllable by the staff but accessible to children,
   where the children may pick out a book or game to
   settle individually or in small groups to enjoy it? ___ ___ ___
   Comments: _____
   _____

7. Are the drinking fountains scaled for children? ___ ___ ___
   Comments: _____
   _____

8. Are there rest rooms scaled for children in the
   children's area? ___ ___ ___
   Comments: _____
   _____

9. Do one or more of the children's rest rooms include
   a diaper-changing table? ___ ___ ___
   Comments: _____
   _____

10. If rest-room facilities are not located in the children's area,
    are they located adjacent to or near the children's area? ___ ___ ___
    Comments: _____
    _____

11. Are there some imaginative pieces of furniture for
    visual surprise? ___ ___ ___
    Comments: _____
    _____

12. Are cheerful colors, interesting geometric shapes, and
    graphic sketches used in the children's area? ___ ___ ___
    Comments: _____
    _____

13. Have sharp corners and edges been eliminated from
    furniture and equipment? ___ ___ ___

	YES	NO	N/A

Comments: _____

_____

14. Are the tabletops, chairs, and floors easily cleaned? ____ ____ ____

Comments: _____

_____

15. Is there comfortable adult seating for use while adults are sharing books with children? ____ ____ ____

Comments: _____

_____

16. Does the staff have visual control of the area? ____ ____ ____

Comments: _____

_____

17. Is realia conveniently and attractively housed? ____ ____ ____

Comments: _____

_____

18. Is there sufficient space for use and secure storage (locked if needed) of audiovisual materials and equipment? ____ ____ ____

Comments: _____

_____

19. Is there sufficient space for crafts activities and storage of crafts materials? ____ ____ ____

Comments: _____

_____

20. Is the floor a single height to allow for flexibility in programming and accessibility, as well as to avoid injuries? ____ ____ ____

Comments: _____

_____

21. Is there a separate programming area adjacent to, but out of, the traffic flow? ____ ____ ____

Comments: _____

_____

22. Is the programming area designed to be multipurpose when not used for special functions, i.e., quiet study, computer resource center, etc.? ____ ____ ____

Comments: _____

_____

	YES	NO	N/A

23. Is the programming area designed to handle the full
    age range of children who use the library?   ____ ____ ____
    Comments: _____
    _____

24. Has allowance been made for storage of special equip-
    ment used in programming, such as a puppet stage?   ____ ____ ____
    Comments: _____
    _____

25. Is the children's area acoustically designed to avoid
    interfering with other library functions?   ____ ____ ____
    Comments: _____
    _____

26. Do interior finishes and materials enhance the acoustics?   ____ ____ ____
    Comments: _____
    _____

27. Are play areas designed to avoid interfering with
    other library functions?   ____ ____ ____
    Comments: _____
    _____

28. Has allowance been provided for specific displays
    and materials geared to children?   ____ ____ ____
    Comments: _____
    _____

29. If children's and adult circulation counters are separated,
    is there lower counter space set aside for children,
    visibly marked by large graphics?   ____ ____ ____
    Comments: _____
    _____

30. Has sufficient space been allowed for easy access by
    children if materials are checked out or returned at
    the children's desk?   ____ ____ ____
    Comments: _____
    _____

	YES	NO	N/A

E. Young Adult Facilities

1. Did a teen advisory panel work with the design team
   in developing the young adult space?   ___ ___ ___

   Comments: _____

   _____

2. Is the location of the young adult area easily determined
   when one enters the library?   ___ ___ ___

   Comments: _____

   _____

3. Is the young adult section separate from other areas
   in the library?   ___ ___ ___

   Comments: _____

   _____

4. Is the space closer to the adult section than to the
   children's section?   ___ ___ ___

   Comments: _____

   _____

5. Does the space encourage young adult use by allowing
   them to "control it" as they control personal space in
   their homes?   ___ ___ ___

   Comments: _____

   _____

6. Is the space slightly secluded, giving the appearance
   of privacy, while still allowing some supervision?   ___ ___ ___

   Comments: _____

   _____

7. Does the space include glassed in and acoustically
   separate seminar rooms that allow group study?   ___ ___ ___

   Comments: _____

   _____

8. Does the space include a glassed in and acoustically
   separate area with a large screen television and audio
   equipment?   ___ ___ ___

   Comments: _____

   _____

9. Do the materials housed in the young adult area appeal
   to the intended audience? Materials such as paperbacks
   in multiple copies arranged as in bookstores, uncluttered

	YES	NO	N/A

shelves, and collections grouped by genre such as science fiction, romances, and mysteries?   ____ ____ ____

Comments: _____

_____

10. Are the shelving and fixtures used to store young adult materials similar to those found in music, video, and bookstores?   ____ ____ ____

Comments: _____

_____

11. Does the space include computers for word processing and spreadsheets, access to the Internet, and games?   ____ ____ ____

Comments: _____

_____

12. Is there secure and adequate space to store teen gear such as skateboards and backpacks?   ____ ____ ____

Comments: _____

_____

13. Does the space allow a variety of comfortable seating options including traditional seating, chairs designed to tilt back without tipping, couches, and floor seating?   ____ ____ ____

Comments: _____

_____

14. Is there space allocated to reflect young adult pride and activities including bulletin boards listing teen accomplishments and activities?   ____ ____ ____

Comments: _____

_____

F. Multimedia Facilities

1. Does the facility provide an opportunity to market multimedia materials and services to users?   ____ ____ ____

Comments: _____

_____

2. Does the media room have a separate, independent heating/cooling system that can be regulated to control the temperature and humidity?   ____ ____ ____

Comments: _____

_____

	YES	NO	N/A

3. Is there special humidifying/dehumidifying equipment to maintain a 60 percent relative humidity?
    Comments: _____

4. Do air conditioning units have electrostatic filters?
    Comments: _____

5. Are supply and return air vents located high on the walls or in the ceiling with air velocities low enough to prevent problems with paper, hair, or clothing?
    Comments: _____

6. Can windows be opened to provide ventilation in case the HVAC system breaks down?
    Comments: _____

7. Is there sufficient acoustical treatment to prevent external noise sources from interfering with listening to media?
    Comments: _____

8. Has the following equipment been considered for placement in multimedia areas:

    a) Audiovisual carrels with built-in playback equipment?

    b) Secured and locked storage cabinets for equipment such as videotape recorders, cassette players, overhead movie and slide projectors, etc.?

    c) Computer workstations and printers?

    d) CD-ROM terminals and printers?

    e) OPAC workstations and printers?

    f) Microform reader/printers?

    g) Podiums?

    h) Public address systems?

    i) Tables?

    j) Chairs?

	YES	NO	N/A
k) Lounge furniture?	___	___	___
l) Shelving for books and media?	___	___	___
m) Televisions?	___	___	___
n) Videotape recorders?	___	___	___
o) Projection television?	___	___	___
p) Moving picture projectors?	___	___	___
q) Screen (wall or rear view)?	___	___	___
r) Compact disc players?	___	___	___
s) Audiocassette players?	___	___	___
t) DVD players?	___	___	___

Comments: _____

9. Does the facility employ an in-the-floor grid system to accommodate and easily change connections for electrical service, television, and communications distribution throughout the multimedia area?   ___ ___ ___

Comments: _____

G. Special Collections/Rare Books/Archives

1. Do the building program and/or institutional guidelines spell out the security necessary in the room?   ___ ___ ___
   Comments: _____

2. Is there a desk strategically located to allow an attendant a clear view of the readers?   ___ ___ ___
   Comments: _____

3. Is the reading room arranged to assure staff observance of those who are exiting?   ___ ___ ___
   Comments: _____

	YES	NO	N/A

4. Are reading tables arranged in open positions, allowing maximum supervision from staff areas?

Comments: _____

_____

5. Are the reading tables generously sized individual tables with task lighting, power for typewriters and/or laptop computers, and table lecterns for holding large books?

Comments: _____

_____

6. Are a few larger tables provided for use of large folios?

Comments: _____

_____

7. Are the rare books housed in locked cases with grilled doors?

Comments: _____

_____

8. Are the rare books shelved in specially designed (padded) bookstacks that are securely braced with earthquake safety devices that prevent books from falling off shelves?

Comments: _____

_____

9. Are manuscripts and archives housed in acid-free boxes?

Comments: _____

_____

10. Are microfilm reading machines and other equipment provided to "read" all of the types of media and materials located in the room?

Comments: _____

_____

11. Are reading and exhibit areas separated?

Comments: _____

_____

12. Can an even temperature of 70 degrees F and humidity of about 50 percent be maintained to prolong the life of the books and materials?

Comments: _____

_____

	YES	NO	N/A

13. Is there an electrostatic filter for the removal of dust and dirt?

Comments: _____

_____

14. In addition, is there a backup mechanical filter should the electrostatic filter break down?

Comments: _____

_____

15. Is the location of the air intake high enough on the exterior wall or roof to avoid chemical and exhaust pollution, especially in urban areas?

Comments: _____

_____

16. Is care taken to control the levels of damaging (especially ultraviolet) light?

Comments: _____

_____

17. Is the area monitored for insects, rodents, and other biological pests which may attack the collection? (Mechanical and/or chemical control techniques can be used.)

Comments: _____

_____

18. Is the area monitored and protected to provide security with:

   a) A vault or strong room?

   b) Special restricted keying and access?

   c) Intrusion alarms?

   d) Door contacts and other forms of perimeter protection?

   e) Monitoring controls and alarms to indicate changes from desired temperature and/or humidity?

   f) Smoke and fire alarms?

   g) Water alarms?

   h) Special alarms in display cases?

   i) Panic alarms for staff?

   j) Security video cameras to monitor the collection and reading areas?

	YES	NO	N/A

Comments: _____

_____

19. Has the library instituted a policy as to how to respond
    to alarms and where their signals should be seen
    or heard?　　　　　　　　　　　　　　　　　　____　　____　　____

    Comments: _____

    _____

20. Is there adequate work space provided for conserva-
    tion work?　　　　　　　　　　　　　　　　　　____　　____　　____

    Comments: _____

    _____

21. Is a disaster preparedness plan in effect?　　____　　____　　____

    Comments: _____

    _____

22. Are disaster supplies stored mainly off-site but with
    a small cache on-site?　　　　　　　　　　　　____　　____　　____

    Comments: _____

    _____

H. Literacy Center

1. Does the library provide a literacy or reading center
   service?　　　　　　　　　　　　　　　　　　　____　　____　　____

   Comments: _____

   _____

2. Is the literacy center a separate room or area in the
   library? (If so, the following questions should
   be asked.)　　　　　　　　　　　　　　　　　　____　　____　　____

   Comments: _____

   _____

3. Are there office space and equipment for the literacy
   program manager?　　　　　　　　　　　　　　____　　____　　____

   Comments: _____

   _____

4. Is space provided for a public bulletin display board
   and brochure rack?　　　　　　　　　　　　　　____　　____　　____

   Comments: _____

   _____

	YES	NO	N/A

5. Is there space for a literacy book collection? ____ ____ ____

   Comments: _____

   _____

6. Are there two-position tutoring study carrels for learner
   and tutor interaction? ____ ____ ____

   Comments: _____

   _____

7. Is there space for computer learning stations? (Each
   station should have seating for two [learner and tutor],
   a computer with appropriate software, and storage
   for software and supplies.) ____ ____ ____

   Comments: _____

   _____

8. Is the lab acoustically controlled so that noise will not
   impact learners using the lab or other areas of the
   learning center? ____ ____ ____

   Comments: _____

   _____

9. Is there a small conference room that might serve as
   a functional office as well as a place for informal
   discussion? ____ ____ ____

   Comments: _____

   _____

10. Are there workstations or work areas for staff? ____ ____ ____

   Comments: _____

   _____

11. Are there workstations or work areas for volunteers? ____ ____ ____

   Comments: _____

   _____

I. Meeting and Seminar Rooms

1. Is the meeting-room entry close to the main entrance? ____ ____ ____

   Comments: _____

   _____

2. Is there an assembly area adequate in size for handling
   the arrival and departure of large groups that may be
   attending meetings? ____ ____ ____

   Comments: _____

	YES	NO	N/A

3. Can the meeting-room area be closed off from the
    remainder of the library?   ___   ___   ___
    Comments: _____
    _____

4. When the meeting room is closed off from the rest of
    the library, do users have access to public rest rooms?   ___   ___   ___
    Comments: _____
    _____

5. Are floor coverings easy to clean and replace?   ___   ___   ___
    Comments: _____
    _____

6. Will a portable or built-in stage be required?   ___   ___   ___
    Comments: _____
    _____

7. Will a lectern or podium be required?   ___   ___   ___
    Comments: _____
    _____

8. Is there a public telephone that may be used when
    the library is closed?   ___   ___   ___
    Comments: _____
    _____

9. Is there a drinking fountain that may be used when
    the library is closed?   ___   ___   ___
    Comments: _____
    _____

10. If the meeting room is large, is it equipped with fold-
    ing doors that can be used as dividers to split the
    room into two or more parts?   ___   ___   ___
    Comments: _____
    _____

11. If folding partitions are used, can users get to and
    from each meeting room without disturbing those in
    adjacent rooms?   ___   ___   ___
    Comments: _____
    _____

12. Are there provisions for hanging coats?   ___   ___   ___
    Comments: _____

	YES	NO	N/A

13. Does the room provide flexibility to accommodate a variety of programming activities, from children's story hours to film showings to art exhibitions? ____ ____ ____

Comments: _____

_____

14. Are there special lighting fixtures and dimmer switches located in the ceiling above the speaker to provide glare-free and appropriate lighting? ____ ____ ____

Comments: _____

_____

15. Is the lighting controllable in intensity, allowing full darkening of the room for visual presentations? ____ ____ ____

Comments: _____

_____

16. Are window coverings provided to darken the room and block out light for visual presentations? ____ ____ ____

Comments: _____

_____

17. Is there a kitchen for the preparation of food and for serving light refreshments? ____ ____ ____

Comments: _____

_____

18. Are there provisions for lockable pass-through from the kitchen to the meeting room for food and beverage service? ____ ____ ____

Comments: _____

_____

19. Is the kitchen equipped with a sink, garbage disposal, microwave oven, stove, refrigerator, ice maker, and cabinets for storage of dishes and equipment? ____ ____ ____

Comments: _____

_____

20. Is the room appropriately wired for phone, cable, teleconferencing, etc.? ____ ____ ____

Comments: _____

_____

21. Are there electrical and telecommunication outlets

	YES	NO	N/A
on all walls and at needed locations on the floor?	____	____	____

Comments: _____

22. Are adequate space, data lines, and power provided for the following equipment:

a) Overhead projectors? ____ ____ ____

b) Projection from laptop computers? ____ ____ ____

c) 35mm slide projectors? ____ ____ ____

d) Ceiling- or wall-mounted screens? ____ ____ ____

e) Large-screen or projection televisions? ____ ____ ____

f) Videocassette recorders? ____ ____ ____

g) Video DVD player? ____ ____ ____

h) Teleconferencing equipment? ____ ____ ____

i) Audio sound system using radio, audiocassettes, and compact discs? ____ ____ ____

j) Public-address system? ____ ____ ____

k) Wireless microphones? ____ ____ ____

l) Podium with links to the various sound systems? ____ ____ ____

m) Personal computers? ____ ____ ____

n) Satellite-dish equipment? ____ ____ ____

Comments: _____

23. Is there lockable storage for equipment? ____ ____ ____

Comments: _____

24. Are there blackboards and/or white marker boards? ____ ____ ____

Comments: _____

25. Are there art rails for exhibitions? ____ ____ ____

Comments: _____

26. Are the meeting-room chairs stackable? ____ ____ ____

Comments: _____

	YES	NO	N/A

27. Are caddies available to move and store the chairs?   ____   ____   ____
    Comments: _____
    _____

28. Are the tables folding?   ____   ____   ____
    Comments: _____
    _____

29. Does the folding mechanism of the tables operate easily?   ____   ____   ____
    Comments: _____
    _____

30. Do the tables have:

    a) Fixed-height bases?   ____   ____   ____

    b) Adjustable-height bases?   ____   ____   ____

    Comments: _____
    _____

31. Are caddies available to store and move the tables?   ____   ____   ____
    Comments: _____
    _____

32. Are the chairs and tables light enough to be moved
    and maneuvered by library staff?   ____   ____   ____
    Comments: _____
    _____

33. Are there lockable storage areas near meeting rooms
    for audiovisual equipment and/or furniture such as
    lecterns or stackable chairs?   ____   ____   ____
    Comments: _____
    _____

34. Have provisions been made to prevent noisy programs
    from interfering with library operations?   ____   ____   ____
    Comments: _____
    _____

J. Convenience Facilities

1. Are rest rooms located close to the lobby or building
   entrance?   ____   ____   ____

	YES	NO	N/A

Comments: _____

_____

2. Does every floor have rest rooms for both men and women? ___ ___ ___

Comments: _____

_____

3. Are rest rooms easily identified? ___ ___ ___

Comments: _____

_____

4. Are there special rest rooms for children, located in or near the children's area? ___ ___ ___

Comments: _____

_____

5. Do all rest rooms contain an area for changing children's diapers? ___ ___ ___

Comments: _____

_____

6. Does every floor have a drinking fountain? ___ ___ ___

Comments: _____

_____

7. Are there drinking fountains for children? ___ ___ ___

Comments: _____

_____

8. Are public telephones available? ___ ___ ___

Comments: _____

_____

9. Are telephones strategically located to encourage convenient use while preventing disturbance to other customers? ___ ___ ___

Comments: _____

_____

10. Are telephone directories provided? ___ ___ ___

Comments: _____

_____

11. Is space allocated for public access to:

a) Photocopiers? ___ ___ ___

b) Telefacsimile (fax) machines? ___ ___ ___

	YES	NO	N/A

c) Personal computers? ___ ___ ___

d) Computer printers? ___ ___ ___

e) Audiovisual equipment? ___ ___ ___

f) Other? ___ ___ ___

Comments: _____

_____

12. Are signs available identifying these machines? ___ ___ ___
Comments: _____

_____

13. Are coin-changing machines located near these machines? ___ ___ ___
Comments: _____

_____

14. Are provisions made for noise abatement in noisy areas of the library? ___ ___ ___
Comments: _____

_____

15. Are provisions made for trash and recycling? ___ ___ ___
Comments: _____

_____

16. Is there a refreshment area available for the public? ___ ___ ___
Comments: _____

_____

17. Are vending machines available for public use? ___ ___ ___
Comments: _____

_____

18. Is the refreshment area located away from public service areas? ___ ___ ___
Comments: _____

_____

19. Is the refreshment area easily viewed and supervised by staff? ___ ___ ___
Comments: _____

_____

20. Are trash receptacles available? ___ ___ ___
Comments: _____

	YES	NO	N/A

21. Are clocks strategically located and visible in every major public area?
    _____ _____ _____
    Comments: _____

22. Are the clocks easily accessible for resetting the time? _____ _____ _____
    Comments: _____

23. If smoking is permitted, are smoking areas clearly identified?
    _____ _____ _____
    Comments: _____

24. Is there a separate elevator for staff? _____ _____ _____
    Comments: _____

25. Is there a separate elevator for freight? _____ _____ _____
    Comments: _____

K. Library Store

If a library store is provided,

1. Is the store in a prominent location to attract the attention of customers as they walk by?
    _____ _____ _____
    Comments: _____

2. Are there adequate signage, window displays, and other visual cues to draw potential customers?
    _____ _____ _____
    Comments: _____

3. Are the circulation paths simple and logical? (Customers should be able to concentrate on the merchandise and not be worried about bumping into things.)
    _____ _____ _____

	YES	NO	N/A

Comments: _____
_____

4. Is the cash/wrapping counter designed and located for maximum efficiency, accessibility, and optimal equipment placement?　　　____　　____　　____

Comments: _____
_____

5. Is there a cash register?　　　____　　____　　____

Comments: _____
_____

6. Is there an office/storage room located in the store?　　____　　____　　____

Comments: _____
_____

7. Is the design of the display fixtures flexible to permit new products to be added periodically?　　　____　　____　　____

Comments: _____
_____

8. Will some products require special displays or display techniques?　　　____　　____　　____

Comments: _____
_____

9. Is a specific lighting source (incandescent, fluorescent, or halogen) preferred?　　　____　　____　　____

Comments:_____
_____

10. Are there security systems in place to protect staff, merchandise, and cash?　　　____　　____　　____

Comments: _____
_____

11. Are there special requirements for cooling or heating any areas of the store?　　　____　　____　　____

Comments: _____
_____

12. Are telephones required?　　　____　　____　　____

Comments: _____
_____

13. Are there enough electrical outlets?　　　____　　____　　____

	YES	NO	N/A

Comments: _____

_____

14. Will the store have a sound system?　　　　　　　____　　____　　____

Comments: _____

_____

15. Are there preferred materials for the walls?　　　____　　____　　____

Comments: _____

_____

16. Are there preferred materials for the floors?　　　____　　____　　____

Comments: _____

_____

17. Are there preferred materials for the ceiling?　　　____　　____　　____

Comments: _____

_____

L. Displays

1. Are the display furnishings and shelving appropriate
   for merchandising the library's products and services?　____　____　____

   Comments: _____

   _____

2. Can library materials be arranged in an attractive,
   appealing way to promote library products?　　　　____　____　____

   Comments: _____

   _____

3. Does the display shelving have built-in signs, boards,
   and lights to draw the attention of the library user?　____　____　____

   Comments: _____

   _____

4. Are the racks for displaying audiovisual materials
   stable when filled?　　　　　　　　　　　　　____　____　____

   Comments: _____

   _____

5. Are there bulletin boards for community notices and
   activities?　　　　　　　　　　　　　　　　____　____　____

	YES	NO	N/A

Comments: _____

_____

6. Are there secure and locked exhibit cases, both free-standing and built-in?   ___   ___   ___

Comments: _____

_____

7. Do the cases have lighting to highlight the exhibits?   ___   ___   ___

Comments: _____

_____

8. Do the cases have surfaces that make posting easy?   ___   ___   ___

Comments: _____

_____

9. Are the cases ventilated to avoid overheating and damaging the exhibits?   ___   ___   ___

Comments: _____

_____

10. Are display cases located in high traffic areas to make these areas more visually interesting?   ___   ___   ___

Comments: _____

_____

11. Is there space for the distribution of community information, tax forms, flyers, and other handouts?   ___   ___   ___

Comments: _____

_____

12. Is there a clear modular system of racks and displays for distribution of community notices and giveaway items to prevent clutter?   ___   ___   ___

Comments: _____

_____

13. Are the racks and displays for distributing materials flexible enough to handle a variety of sizes and shapes of literature in a neat, attractive manner?   ___   ___   ___

Comments: _____

_____

14. Are the racks displayed in highly visible locations in order to attract customers and merchandise materials?   ___   ___   ___

Comments: _____

_____

	YES	NO	N/A

M. Interior Signage

1. Do signs meet ADA requirements (see section 5)?
   Comments: _____
   _____

2. Has the sign system been integrated into the building design and furniture selection process (architecture, color, etc.)?
   Comments: _____
   _____

3. Is there consistency in signage throughout the building? (Signs that serve the same function throughout the building should have the same shape, size, layout, type size, and placement.)
   Comments: _____
   _____

4. Are the signs of good design? (Typeface, size, spacing of letters, contrast, use of symbols, and color should all be considered.)
   Comments: _____
   _____

5. Are the sizes of signs proportional to distance from users and are signs sequentially positioned to facilitate self-service?
   Comments: _____
   _____

6. Are the signs well lighted, easy to read, and positioned for a clear view?
   Comments: _____
   _____

7. Do signs use terminology consistently? (Only one term should be applied to any one area, service, etc.)
   Comments: _____
   _____

8. Is the text of the sign clearly and accurately written in order to communicate the intended message effectively and positively?
   Comments: _____
   _____

	YES	NO	N/A

9. Is the signage system flexible enough that, as conditions change, signs can be changed or moved easily?   ____   ____   ____

Comments: _____

_____

10. Is redundancy avoided? (Too many signs, all providing the same message, can be as bad as no sign at all.)   ____   ____   ____

Comments: _____

_____

11. Are signs positioned and designed to avoid injuries (sharp corners, height, etc.)?   ____   ____   ____

Comments: _____

_____

12. Are signs reasonably vandal proof?   ____   ____   ____

Comments: _____

_____

13. Is the exterior monument sign(s) identifying the library positioned so that it is easy to read when approaching the library? (A sign perpendicular to the road is easier to read than a sign parallel to the road.)   ____   ____   ____

Comments: _____

_____

14. Is there a directory identifying major library services and their locations?   ____   ____   ____

Comments: _____

_____

15. Are directional signs available leading patrons to different departments and placed at logical decision points?   ____   ____   ____

Comments: _____

_____

16. Are there signs on doors and at the entrances to departments to identify the function or service within that room or area?   ____   ____   ____

Comments: _____

_____

17. Are there signs to highlight temporary collections and services or to announce events taking place in the library?   ____   ____   ____

Comments: _____

_____

	YES	NO	N/A

18. Are there signs that can be easily changed on the end panels of stacks to identify which books are shelved in that range?

    Comments: _____

_____

19. Are there signs to provide critical information about regulations, warnings, procedures, instructions, and hours?

    Comments: _____

_____

20. Are instructional signs available for catalog use?

    Comments: _____

_____

N. Workroom/Offices

1. Are there individual workstations for all staff?

    Comments: _____

_____

2. Are there adequate workstations for library volunteers?

    Comments: _____

_____

3. Are workstations free from distractions?

    Comments: _____

_____

4. When required for team activities, are some workstations designed to foster communication among staff?

    Comments: _____

_____

5. Are there lockers and/or coat closets where personal items can be stored and secured for staff and volunteers?

    Comments: _____

_____

6. Is there adequate at-hand storage space?

    Comments: _____

_____

	YES	NO	N/A

7. Is there a sick-bay area or a place where ill staff
members may rest?   ___   ___   ___

Comments: _____

_____

8. Is there adequate space for equipment such as personal
computers, terminals, word processors, television/VCR
units with stands?   ___   ___   ___

Comments: _____

_____

9. Is there adequate space for a variety of types of library
storage?   ___   ___   ___

Comments: _____

_____

10. Is there a locking storage unit or area to secure valuable equipment such as CD players, slide projectors,
cameras, etc.?   ___   ___   ___

Comments: _____

_____

11. Is there a locking storage unit to secure media and
other expensive items during processing and prior to
delivery to the public shelves?   ___   ___   ___

Comments: _____

_____

12. Is there adequate space for technical services operations? ___   ___   ___

Comments: _____

_____

13. Are adequate work counters present to handle all tasks
assigned to the workroom?   ___   ___   ___

Comments: _____

_____

14. Are there adequate sorting shelves for the storage of
returned library items?   ___   ___   ___

Comments: _____

_____

15. Is there a smart terminal connected to library databases
with a printer in the workroom to check in library items
and look up the records for donated items?   ___   ___   ___

	YES	NO	N/A

Comments: _____

_____

16. Is there a typewriter in addition to the computer
terminal?

Comments: _____

_____

17. Are there telephones?

Comments: _____

_____

18. Are there enough electrical outlets for all required
equipment?

Comments: _____

_____

19. Are there enough data lines?

Comments: _____

_____

20. Is there adequate space for book trucks at workstations
and for their storage when not in use?

Comments: _____

_____

21. Is the work-flow pattern effective and conducive to
staff productivity?

Comments: _____

_____

22. Are environmental conditions such as lighting, HVAC,
and acoustics adequate and comfortable?

Comments: _____

_____

23. Is the manager's office separate, in an enclosed room,
to ensure privacy?

Comments: _____

_____

24. Is there a personal computer in the manager's office
for typing evaluations and other confidential types
of materials?

Comments: _____

_____

	YES	NO	N/A

25. Does the public have convenient access to the manager's office?

Comments: _____

_____

26. Does the manager have convenient access to the workroom from his or her office?

Comments: _____

_____

27. Are there provisions for U.S. mail and newspaper delivery when the library is closed?

Comments: _____

_____

O. Staff Lounge

1. Are there lockers and/or coat closets where personal items can be stored and secured for staff and volunteers?

Comments: _____

_____

2. Is there a kitchen for the preparation of food and for serving light refreshments?

Comments: _____

_____

3. Is the kitchen equipped with a sink, garbage disposal, microwave oven, stove, refrigerator, ice maker, and cabinets for storage of dishes and equipment?

Comments: _____

_____

4. Is there provision for a ventilating system to eliminate strong food odors?

Comments: _____

_____

5. Are there vending machines for food and soft drinks?

Comments: _____

_____

6. Are there tables and chairs?

Comments: _____

_____

	YES	NO	N/A

7. Is there a cot/sofa that can be used by the staff
or customers in case of an emergency? _____ _____ _____
   Comments: _____
   _____

8. Is there a window to look out on a quiet, pleasant scene? _____ _____ _____
   Comments: _____
   _____

9. Does the staff have separate rest rooms from the public? _____ _____ _____
   Comments: _____
   _____

10. Is the staff lounge acoustically treated to eliminate
the transfer of sound to and from adjacent public and
staff areas? _____ _____ _____
   Comments: _____
   _____

P. Friends of the Library

1. Does the library have a Friends of the Library group? _____ _____ _____
   Comments: _____
   _____

2. Do the Friends of the Library accept donations such as
books (used/new) and other items (puzzles, magazines,
audiovisual)? _____ _____ _____
   Comments: _____
   _____

3. Do the Friends of the Library have their own counter
or work table to sort donated items? _____ _____ _____
   Comments: _____
   _____

4. Do the Friends of the Library have equipment such as
carts and dollies available to handle large donations of
books and media? _____ _____ _____
   Comments: _____
   _____

	YES	NO	N/A

5. Do the Friends of the Library have convenient storage for the above equipment and cardboard boxes for packing the donated items?

Comments: _____

6. Are the donations placed on shelves on the premises so the staff can view and select whatever they want to add to their collection, send to the branch book exchange, or sell?

Comments: _____

7. Is there storage space either on or off the premises for the donated items?

Comments: _____

8. Do the Friends of the Library operate a retail store?

Comments: _____

9. Do the Friends have an:

   a) Annual book sale?

   b) Ongoing daily book sale?

Comments: _____

10. If the Friends have an ongoing daily sale, do they sell their items from:

   a) A store?

   b) Some shelves in the library?

   c) A book cart?

   d) An area adjacent to their room?

Comments: _____

11. Is the book sale area clearly marked by signs?

Comments: _____

12. Is the cash from the Friends' sales kept in a separate place so as not to get confused with the daily cash

	YES	NO	N/A

from fines, etc.? ____ ____ ____

Comments: _____

_____

13. Is there space in a prominent area allotted to the Friends
for their newsletter and membership applications? ____ ____ ____

*Comments:*_____

_____

14. Do the Friends have a mail slot to receive their membership applications, dues, donations, etc.? ____ ____ ____

Comments: _____

_____

15. Do the Friends have a bulletin board for messages? ____ ____ ____

Comments: _____

_____

16. Do the Friends have some space in the staff lounge to
hang their coats and lockers or some other safe place
to store their valuables? ____ ____ ____

Comments: _____

_____

Q. Interior Storage

1. Has storage been considered in planning the library? ____ ____ ____

Comments: _____

_____

2. Is there a room to store pieces of furniture, equipment,
displays, and other miscellaneous items? ____ ____ ____

Comments: _____

_____

3. Is there storage space for less frequently used library
materials such as old newspapers, periodicals, and
donated books awaiting review for possible addition
to the collections? ____ ____ ____

Comments: _____

_____

4. Is there adequate storage for office and library supplies? ____ ____ ____

Comments: _____

_____

	YES	NO	N/A

5. Is there another building on library property where infrequently used materials can be stored to make room for rapidly growing collections? ___ ___ ___

   Comments: _____

   _____

6. Is off-site storage available? ___ ___ ___

   Comments: _____

   _____

7. Is there a policy in place to keep the storage area from becoming the library's "attic"? ___ ___ ___

   Comments: _____

   _____

R. Remote Storage Facilities

1. Has an off-site storage facility been considered as a place to house secondary or little used materials? ___ ___ ___

   Comments: _____

   _____

2. Is the facility a cold-storage warehouse that maximizes the use of space through high-density shelving? ___ ___ ___

   Comments: _____

   _____

3. Does the facility have high ceilings to allow for tall, adjustable, open rack shelving? ___ ___ ___

   Comments: _____

   _____

4. Has a policy decision been made to store materials by size or by subject classifications? ___ ___ ___

   Comments: _____

   _____

5. Is there space for processing in the facility? ___ ___ ___

   Comments: _____

   _____

6. Is there space for reading by customers who may visit the remote storage building? ___ ___ ___

   Comments: _____

	YES	NO	N/A

7. Is there a high security area for special collections?
   _Comments:_____

8. Is the location of stored materials linked through
   barcodes or inventory control numbers to the
   library's catalog?
   _Comments:_____

9. If stored materials are not linked to the library's
   catalog, is there an inventory control system used
   at the storage facility to easily locate and retrieve
   materials?
   _Comments:_____

10. Are materials stored in an environment of approxi-
    mately 55 to 65 degrees F and 40 to 55 percent
    relative humidity?
    _Comments:_____

11. Are constant environmental conditions maintained
    throughout the year?
    _Comments:_____

12. Is low lighting (sodium vapor or fluorescent light
    fixtures with UV shields) used in order to reduce
    the damage that light does to books?
    _Comments:_____

13. Is the amount of time that lights are left on kept
    to a minimum?
    _Comments:_____

14. Has a delivery system been established for quick
    access to the stored collections for library customers?
    _Comments:_____

5 ✓✓✓ Compliance with ADA Accessibility Guidelines

In addition to the guidelines listed below, please check state and local codes and regulations, as well as the Americans with Disabilities Act of 1990 (ADA).

	YES	NO	N/A

A. Parking, Curb Cuts, and Ramps

1. Are there safe and accessible parking spaces located on the shortest accessible route of travel to an accessible entrance?   ___   ___   ___

   *Comments:*_____

   _____

2. Do accessible parking spaces have a designated sign showing the symbol of accessibility?   ___   ___   ___

   *Comments:*_____

   _____

3. Are the accessible parking spaces at least 8 feet wide and 20 feet long?   ___   ___   ___

   *Comments:*_____

   _____

4. Is 1 in every 8 accessible parking spaces, but not less than 1 overall, served by an access aisle 96 inches in width with signage which indicates "Van Accessible" under the accessibility symbol?   ___   ___   ___

   *Comments:*_____

   _____

	YES	NO	N/A

5. Are access aisles between van parking spaces 5 feet in width, striped, and part of an accessible route? (Two accessible parking spaces can share a common access aisle.)   ___   ___   ___

Comments:_____

_____

6. Does the van-accessible parking space clear vertically to at least 9 feet 6 inches high?   ___   ___   ___

Comments:_____

_____

7. If the library has a passenger-loading zone, does the zone have an access aisle 5 feet wide and 20 feet long, adjacent and parallel to vehicle pull-up space?   ___   ___   ___

Comments:_____

_____

8. Are there any curbs between the access aisle and the vehicle pull-up space? If so, are there cuts or curb ramps?   ___   ___   ___

Comments:_____

_____

9. Are the accessible parking lot spaces and aisles level so that wheelchairs will not roll if left unattended while transferring persons to their vehicle?   ___   ___   ___

Comments:_____

_____

10. If the pavement is not level, is the slope no more than 2 percent in all directions?   ___   ___   ___

Comments:_____

_____

11. Does the facility observe the following requirements for parking spaces?   ___   ___   ___

No. of Spaces	Minimum Accessible Spaces
1 to 100	1 for each 1–25 spaces
101 to 200	4 + 1 for each 1–50 spaces
201 to 500	6 + 1 for each 1–100 spaces
501 to 1,000	2 percent of total spaces
1,001 and over	20 + 1 for each 1–100 over 1,000

Comments:_____

_____

	YES	NO	N/A

12. Are there curb cuts or curb ramps at all curbs and walks on accessible routes to accessible entrances? ____ ____ ____

    *Comments:*_____

    _____

13. Do the curb cuts or curb ramps provide drainage so that water will not be trapped after a storm? ____ ____ ____

    *Comments:*_____

    _____

14. Do curb cuts or curb ramps have a slope of 1:12 or less and flared sides with a slope of 1:10? ____ ____ ____

    *Comments:*_____

    _____

15. If there are curb ramps, are they built so they do not extend into vehicle traffic lanes? ____ ____ ____

    *Comments:*_____

    _____

16. Are curb cuts or ramps 36 inches wide excluding the flared sides? ____ ____ ____

    *Comments:*_____

    _____

17. Is the slope of all exterior walkways 1:12 or less? ____ ____ ____

    *Comments:*_____

    _____

18. Do the ramps:

    a) Have a minimum clear width of 36 inches? ____ ____ ____

    b) Have level landings at the top and bottom, at least as wide as the ramp? ____ ____ ____

    c) Have landings at least 60 inches in length? ____ ____ ____

    *Comments:*_____

    _____

19. If the ramp changes direction, is the landing at least 60 inches by 60 inches? ____ ____ ____

    *Comments:*_____

    _____

	YES	NO	N/A

20. If the slope of the ramp is

    a) Between 1:12 and 1:16, does the ramp have a level landing 60 inches in length at 30-foot intervals?   ___   ___   ___

    b) Between 1:16 and 1:20, does the ramp have level landings 60 inches in length at 40-foot intervals?   ___   ___   ___

    *Comments:*_____

21. Is the cross slope of all ramps and walks 1:50 or less?   ___   ___   ___

    *Comments:*_____

22. If the ramp

    a) Has a rise (i.e., a height of 6 inches or more), does the ramp have handrails on both sides?   ___   ___   ___

    b) Is 6 feet or more in length, does the ramp have handrails on both sides?   ___   ___   ___

    *Comments:*_____

23. Are stairs at least 36 inches in width?   ___   ___   ___

    *Comments:*_____

24. Are all the steps on any given flight of stairs uniform in height and depth?   ___   ___   ___

    *Comments:*_____

25. Are stair depths no less than 11 inches?   ___   ___   ___

    *Comments:*_____

26. Are the nosings (the usually rounded edge of a stair tread that extends over the riser) rounded or curved?   ___   ___   ___

    *Comments:*_____

27. Do the nosings project no more than 1.5 inches past the riser of the step?   ___   ___   ___

    *Comments:*_____

	YES	NO	N/A

28. Do stairways have handrails on both sides?   ____   ____   ____
    Comments: _____

    _____

29. Is the diameter or width of the gripping surface of
    the handrail 1.25 inches to 1.5 inches?   ____   ____   ____
    Comments: _____

    _____

30. If the handrail is located adjacent to a wall, is the space
    between the handrail and wall at least 1.5 inches?   ____   ____   ____
    Comments: _____

    _____

31. If the ramp or stairs has a change of direction, is the
    inside handrail continuous?   ____   ____   ____
    Comments: _____

    _____

32. Does the handrail extend at least 12 inches beyond
    the top for stairs, and 12 inches beyond the top and
    bottom for ramps?   ____   ____   ____
    Comments: _____

    _____

33. Are the extended sections parallel to the surface
    of the landing for ramps and floor for the top step
    of stairs?   ____   ____   ____
    Comments: _____

    _____

34. Does the handrail extend the depth of one tread plus
    12 inches past the bottom step for stairs?   ____   ____   ____
    Comments: _____

    _____

35. Does the handrail extension for stairs slope with the
    bottom step for the distance of one tread depth and
    is the 12-inch extension parallel to the floor?   ____   ____   ____
    Comments: _____

    _____

36. Is the top of the handrail-gripping surface between
    34 inches and 38 inches above the ramps or steps?   ____   ____   ____

	YES	NO	N/A

Comments:_____

_____

37. Are the ends of handrails for ramps and stairs rounded or returning smoothly to the floor or landing? ____ ____ ____

Comments:_____

_____

38. If there is an outside book return, is it accessible to the disabled? ____ ____ ____

Comments:_____

_____

B. Entrances

1. Are all building entrances accessible to the disabled? ____ ____ ____

Comments:_____

_____

2. Are there automatic doors or easy-open doors at the entrance provided for wheelchair access? ____ ____ ____

Comments:_____

_____

3. Do all accessible entrance doors display a sign or sticker with the symbol for accessibility? ____ ____ ____

Comments:_____

_____

4. If some entrances are not accessible, are signs displayed directing people to accessible entrances? ____ ____ ____

Comments:_____

_____

5. Do work areas have an accessible approach, entrance, and exit for persons with disability? ____ ____ ____

Comments:_____

_____

6. Does the accessible entrance door open with a single effort? ____ ____ ____

Comments:_____

_____

	YES	NO	N/A

7. If turnstiles are used in the entrance, is an alternative entrance provided?

   *Comments:*_____

_____

8. Do library security gates have a clear minimum opening of 32 inches?

   *Comments:*_____

_____

9. Do all accessible entrance doors have a clear opening of at least 32 inches?

   *Comments:*_____

_____

10. If double-leaf doors are used, and if only one door is opened, is there a clear space of at least 32 inches?

   *Comments:*_____

_____

11. If the accessible entrance door pulls to open is there a level approach 60 inches in depth from the door?

   *Comments:*_____

_____

12. If the accessible entrance door pushes in to open is there a level approach 48 inches in depth?

   *Comments:*_____

_____

13. If there are two doors in a series and the doors open in the same direction (e.g., both push), are there 48 inches of clear floor space from the first opened door to the door frame of the second door?

   *Comments:*_____

_____

14. If there are two doors in a series and the doors open in opposite directions (one pulling, the second pushing), are there 48 inches of clear space between the doors when they are closed?

   *Comments:*_____

_____

	YES	NO	N/A

15. Are thresholds of doorways half an inch or less? _____ _____ _____

    *Comments:*_____

_____

16. Is the door-opening hardware centered at least
    48 inches from the floor? _____ _____ _____

    *Comments:*_____

_____

C. Accessible Routes within the Building

1. Is there at least one accessible route connecting
   accessible buildings, facilities, elements, and spaces? _____ _____ _____

   *Comments:*_____

_____

2. Are there protruding objects (e.g., telephones, drinking
   fountains, and/or furniture) along these travel routes? _____ _____ _____

   *Comments:*_____

_____

3. If there are any protruding objects with their lead
   edges at or below 27 inches, do they leave a clear
   minimum path of 36 inches? _____ _____ _____

   *Comments:*_____

_____

4. Do these travel routes have a clear minimum width
   of at least 36 inches? _____ _____ _____

   *Comments:*_____

_____

5. If the accessible route is less than 5 feet in width, are
   there passing spaces of 5 feet at intervals of not more
   than 200 feet? _____ _____ _____

   *Comments:*_____

_____

6. Does the facility have a clear space of 64 inches to allow
   two-way passing wheelchair traffic? _____ _____ _____

   *Comments:*_____

_____

	YES	NO	N/A

7. Are there at least 5-foot-by-5-foot passing spaces at 200-foot intervals along these routes?
   _____ _____ _____

   *Comments:*_____

   _____

8. Is there headroom clearance of at least 80 inches above the floor along these routes?
   _____ _____ _____

   *Comments:*_____

   _____

9. Are there T-shaped clearances 5 feet by 5 feet to maneuver wheelchairs?
   _____ _____ _____

   *Comments:*_____

   _____

D. Interior Doors

1. Is the opening hardware centered at 48 inches above the floor?
   _____ _____ _____

   *Comments:*_____

   _____

2. Are there easy-to-grip door handles using push-type, lever-operated, or U-type handles?
   _____ _____ _____

   *Comments:*_____

   _____

3. Do doors open easily?
   _____ _____ _____

   *Comments:*_____

   _____

4. Can doors be pulled or pushed open using a maximum force of 5 pounds?
   _____ _____ _____

   *Comments:*_____

   _____

5. Do accessible doors allow delay closing action of at least 3 seconds to move from an open position to 70 degrees?
   _____ _____ _____

   *Comments:*_____

   _____

6. Do doors open at a 90-degree angle?
   _____ _____ _____

   *Comments:*_____

   _____

	YES	NO	N/A

7. Do doors open clear at least 32 inches from the face of the door to the opposite door stop?

Comments:_____

_____

8. Do doorways have at least a 32-inch clear opening?

Comments:_____

_____

9. Are thresholds raised less than .5 inch from the floor?

Comments:_____

_____

10. Are thresholds for any sliding doors not more than .75 inch from the floor?

Comments:_____

_____

11. Is the operating hardware of fully opened sliding doors exposed and useable from both sides of the door?

Comments:_____

_____

E. Surfaces

1. Are slip-resistant floors used throughout the building?

Comments:_____

_____

2. Are floor surfaces stable and firm?

Comments:_____

_____

3. Are carpets securely attached to the floor?

Comments:_____

_____

4. Are floor surfaces level?

a) If floor-level changes are more than .25 inch and less than .5 inch, is the floor beveled with a slope of 1:2?

	YES	NO	N/A

b) If the change of level is greater than .5 inch (in which case it must be considered a ramp), does it comply with ramp regulations? ____ ____ ____

*Comments:*_____

_____

5. Are floor designators placed at the correct level for persons in wheelchairs? ____ ____ ____

*Comments:*_____

_____

6. Is there clear and distinct contrast between the floor and walls to assist the visually impaired? ____ ____ ____

*Comments:*_____

_____

7. Can a visually disabled individual who is using a cane detect objects protruding from the wall or floor? ____ ____ ____

*Comments:*_____

_____

8. Are objects, appliances, and furniture placed 27 inches off the floor or ground to help cane users? ____ ____ ____

*Comments:*_____

_____

F. Lifts and Elevators

1. If the building has more than one floor, does the wheelchair user have access to an elevator? ____ ____ ____

*Comments:*_____

_____

2. Is the elevator on an accessible route? ____ ____ ____

*Comments:*_____

_____

3. Do the elevators open level with the floor? ____ ____ ____

*Comments:*_____

_____

4. Call buttons:

a) Are they centered 42 inches above the floor? ____ ____ ____

	YES	NO	N/A

b) Do they have a visual signal when a call is registered and answered? ____ ____ ____

c) Is the button at least .75 an inch at its smallest dimension? ____ ____ ____

Comments:_____

5. Hall lanterns:

a) Are they mounted 72 inches to the centerline above the floor? ____ ____ ____

b) Do they have a visual and audible signal? ____ ____ ____

c) Are visual elements at least 2.5 inches at their smallest dimension? ____ ____ ____

Comments:_____

6. Floor designators:

a) Are they located on both doorjambs 60 inches on centerline above the floor?

b) Do they contain raised numbers 2 inches high, with Braille for all floors? ____ ____ ____

Comments:_____

7. Doors:

a) Do they have 36 inches of clear space? ____ ____ ____

b) Do they open and close automatically? ____ ____ ____

c) Do they remain open at least 3 seconds? ____ ____ ____

d) If obstructed, do they remain open for at least 20 seconds before closing? ____ ____ ____

Comments:_____

8. Elevator cars:

a) Do they have an automatic self-leveling feature? ____ ____ ____

b) Do they provide clear floor space 54 inches by 68 inches to allow wheelchair users to maneuver? ____ ____ ____

	YES	NO	N/A

c) Do they have an audible/visual car position indicator? ___ ___ ___

*Comments:*_____

_____

9. Control panels:

a) Are buttons at least .75 inch in smallest dimensions? ___ ___ ___

b) Are buttons designated by Braille, along with raised alphabet and numbers? ___ ___ ___

c) Do buttons provide visual indicators? ___ ___ ___

d) Are buttons no higher than 54 inches? ___ ___ ___

e) Are emergency controls grouped at the bottom with centerlines no less than 35 inches? ___ ___ ___

*Comments:*_____

_____

G. Drinking Fountains

1. If there is more than one drinking fountain per floor, are 50 percent accessible to individuals in wheelchairs? ___ ___ ___
   *Comments:*_____

   _____

2. Are drinking fountains at lower heights (27 to 36 inches) available for wheelchair users and convenient for heights of all users? ___ ___ ___
   *Comments:*_____

   _____

3. Are the spouts on all drinking fountains no higher than 36 inches measured from the floor to the spout? ___ ___ ___
   *Comments:*_____

   _____

4. Are the spouts at the front of the unit within 3 inches of the front edge? ___ ___ ___
   *Comments:*_____

   _____

	YES	NO	N/A

5. Does the water flow at least 4 inches high above the spout so a cup or glass can be placed under the water flow?

    *Comments:*_____

6. Are the controls located on the front, or if side mounted, within 7 inches of the front edge?

    *Comments:*_____

7. Are the controls operable with one hand, and do they operate without an uncomfortable grasping, pinching, or twisting of the wrist?

    *Comments:*_____

8. If the accessible water fountain is wall or post mounted and has knee space, is the space at least 27 inches high, 30 inches wide, and 17 to 19 inches deep?

    *Comments:*_____

9. Is there clear floor space of at least 30 inches wide and 48 inches long in front of the accessible water fountain?

    *Comments:*_____

H. Rest Rooms—General

1. Are rest rooms located on an accessible route?

    *Comments:*_____

2. Are there signs indicating the nearest toilet available for persons with disability?

    *Comments:*_____

3. Is the rest room marked with Braille signage?

    *Comments:*_____

	YES	NO	N/A

4. Is there at least one bathroom accessible for persons
   with disability? ____ ____ ____

   *Comments:*_____

   _____

5. Is the door into the rest room easily opened by the
   disabled? ____ ____ ____

   *Comments:*_____

   _____

6. Are sink pipes either insulated or enclosed to protect
   against contact? ____ ____ ____

   *Comments:*_____

   _____

7. Are sinks no more than 34 inches above the floor? ____ ____ ____

   *Comments:*_____

   _____

8. Is there a knee space under the sink 29 inches to the
   floor and 8 inches deep (from the front rim of the sink)? ____ ____ ____

   *Comments:*_____

   _____

9. Are faucets operable with one hand? ____ ____ ____

   *Comments:*_____

   _____

10. Can faucets be operated with no more than
    5 lbf (pound-force)? ____ ____ ____

    *Comments:*_____

    _____

11. Are faucets positioned to avoid dripping on floors? ____ ____ ____

    *Comments:*_____

    _____

12. Are faucets positioned so as not to interfere with traffic
    or cause injury? ____ ____ ____

    *Comments:*_____

    _____

13. Are mirrors mounted with the bottom edge no more
    than 40 inches above the floor? ____ ____ ____

	YES	NO	N/A

*Comments:*_____

_____

14. Are other fixtures in the rest room (soap dispensers, towels, auto-dryers, sanitary-napkin dispensers, waste-paper receptacles, etc.) located so the controls or dispensers are at a maximum of 48 inches from the floor? ____ ____ ____
    *Comments:*_____

    _____

15. Are coat and purse hooks at a height of approximately 48 inches to make them convenient to wheelchair users? ____ ____ ____
    *Comments:*_____

    _____

I. Rest Rooms with Stalls

1. Is there a minimum clearance of 36 inches between all fixtures to an accessible stall? ____ ____ ____
   *Comments:*_____

   _____

2. Are there 60 inches of clear floor space in the rest room for a wheelchair to make a 180-degree turn? ____ ____ ____
   *Comments:*_____

   _____

3. Is at least one stall accessible to a wheelchair, and does it display the international symbol of accessibility? ____ ____ ____
   *Comments:*_____

   _____

4. Does the immediate area allow 48 inches of clear space to approach the stall door? ____ ____ ____
   *Comments:*_____

   _____

5. Does the door of this stall open out? ____ ____ ____
   *Comments:*_____

   _____

6. Are stall doors at least 32 inches wide? ____ ____ ____
   *Comments:*_____

   _____

	YES	NO	N/A

7. Are stalls at least 60 inches wide? ____ ____ ____

*Comments:*_____

_____

8. Are stalls at least 56 inches in length for a wall-
mounted toilet, and 59 inches in length for a floor-
mounted toilet? ____ ____ ____

*Comments:*_____

_____

9. Are grab bars placed appropriately and where required? ____ ____ ____

*Comments:*_____

_____

10. Are grab bars capable of resisting a force of 250 lbf? ____ ____ ____

*Comments:*_____

_____

11. Are grab bars stable in their fittings? ____ ____ ____

*Comments:*_____

_____

12. Are grab bars between 1.25 and 1.5 inches in diameter? ____ ____ ____

*Comments:*_____

_____

13. Are grab bars free of sharp, abrasive, or protruding
elements? ____ ____ ____

*Comments:*_____

_____

14. Is there at least 1.5 inches of space between grab bars
and the wall? ____ ____ ____

*Comments:*_____

_____

15. Is the toilet-paper holder located within easy reach
from the toilet and at least 19 inches from the floor,
with continuous paper flow? ____ ____ ____

*Comments:*_____

_____

16. Is the toilet seat 17 to 19 inches measured from the
top of the toilet seat to the floor? ____ ____ ____

*Comments:*_____

_____

	YES	NO	N/A

17. Are flush controls either automatic or hand operated? ____ ____ ____

   *Comments:*_____

   _____

18. Are flush valves no more than 44 inches above the floor? ____ ____ ____

   *Comments:*_____

   _____

19. Are flush valves located on the wide side of the toilet? ____ ____ ____

   *Comments:*_____

   _____

20. Are flush valves operable with one hand? ____ ____ ____

   *Comments:*_____

   _____

21. Is toe clearance in the stalls at least 9 inches? ____ ____ ____

   *Comments:*_____

   _____

22. Is the rim of the accessible urinal no more than 17 inches above the floor? ____ ____ ____

   *Comments:*_____

   _____

23. Is there a clear space of at least 30 inches by 48 inches in front of the urinals? ____ ____ ____

   *Comments:*_____

   _____

J. Rest Rooms—Single Rooms

1. Is there a clear floor space of at least 48 inches by 56 inches? ____ ____ ____

   *Comments:*_____

   _____

2. Is the height of the toilet 17 inches to 19 inches measured from the top of the toilet seat to the floor? ____ ____ ____

   *Comments:*_____

   _____

	YES	NO	N/A

3. Are grab bars between 1.25 and 1.5 inches in diameter, with a space of 1.5 inches between the wall and grab bars?

    *Comments:*_____

4. Is there a grab bar behind the toilet at least 36 inches in length and 33 to 36 inches from the floor?

    *Comments:*_____

5. Is there a grab bar on the wall closest to the toilet, 40 inches in length, 33 to 36 inches from the floor, and 12 inches from the back wall?

    *Comments:*_____

6. Are flush valves no more than 44 inches above the floor?

    *Comments:*_____

7. Are flush valves located on the wide side of the toilet?

    *Comments:*_____

8. Are flush valves operable with one hand?

    *Comments:*_____

9. Is the toilet-paper holder located within easy reach from the toilet and at least 19 inches from the floor with continuous paper flow?

    *Comments:*_____

K. Rest Rooms—Unisex

1. Does the rest room comply with the checklist for single-room rest rooms?

    *Comments:*_____

2. Is the accessible unisex rest room located on a wheelchair-accessible route and in the same area as

	YES	NO	N/A

other rest rooms which are not accessible to wheel-chairs?

_Comments:_____

_____

3. Is there signage indicating this is a unisex, wheelchair-accessible rest room?

_Comments:_____

_____

4. Does the unisex rest room have a privacy latch?

_Comments:_____

_____

L. Alarms

1. Are there audible and visual alarm systems?

_Comments:_____

_____

2. If there is an emergency warning system (fire alarms), are visual signal appliances provided in rest rooms and other general usage areas (e.g., meeting rooms, hallways, lobbies, and other areas) for common use?

_Comments:_____

_____

3. Do the visual signal appliances provide a minimum of 75 candlelight?

_Comments:_____

_____

4. Is the visual signal a xenon strobe-type lamp or equivalent?

_Comments:_____

_____

5. Are the visual alarms clear and nominal white?

_Comments:_____

_____

	YES	NO	N/A

6. Are these visual signals flashing at a minimum of 3 Hz with a .2 second duration? ____ ____ ____

   *Comments:*_____

   _____

7. Are these visual signals placed within 50 feet (horizontal plane) of any location within the room? ____ ____ ____

   *Comments:*_____

   _____

8. Are these visual signals within 80 inches above the highest floor level or 6 inches below the ceiling, whichever is lower? ____ ____ ____

   *Comments:*_____

   _____

9. Does the facility have at least one alarm station and one audible system? ____ ____ ____

   *Comments:*_____

   _____

10. Does the facility have an audible alarm which sounds at 15 dBa (decibels above reference noise, adjusted) louder than existing sound levels in the facility? ____ ____ ____

    *Comments:*_____

    _____

11. Do audible alarms have a duration of 60 seconds? ____ ____ ____

    *Comments:*_____

    _____

12. Do audible alarms produce a sound of 15 dBa? ____ ____ ____

    *Comments:*_____

    _____

M. Signage

1. Is large, clearly printed signage provided to identify all areas and functions in the library for the deaf and visually impaired? ____ ____ ____

   *Comments:*_____

   _____

	YES	NO	N/A

2. Do all signs designating permanent rooms and spaces in the building comply with the ADA Accessibility Guidelines for Buildings and Facilities (ADAAG)?

    Comments: _____

3. Does directional and informational signage about functional spaces in the building comply with ADAAG?

    Comments: _____

4. Do all accessible elements (i.e., entrance doors, rest rooms, water fountains, and parking spaces) display the international symbol of accessibility?

    Comments: _____

5. Are the signs placed perpendicular to the route of travel?

    Comments: _____

6. Can permanent signs be approached without encountering a protruding object or standing within the area of a swing door?

    Comments: _____

7. If signs are placed overhead (minimum 80 inches above the floor), are the letters and numbers at least 3 inches in height?

    Comments: _____

8. Are permanent signs for rooms and spaces installed on the wall adjacent to the latch side of the door and mounted at 60 inches above the floor to the centerline of the sign?

    Comments: _____

9. Do all signs that are required to comply with ADAAG have a width-to-height ratio between 3:5 and 1:1 for letters and numbers?

    Comments: _____

	YES	NO	N/A

10. Do the individual letters and numbers of the signs required to comply with ADAAG have a stroke width-to-height ratio between 1:5 and 1:10?

    _Comments:_____

    _____

11. Are Braille markings used throughout the library to enable the blind user to locate access?

    _Comments:_____

    _____

12. Are the letters and numbers of permanent signs:

    a) At least .625 inch but no more than 2 inches in height?

    b) Raised 3 percent per inch?

    c) Accompanied by Grade 2 Braille?

    _Comments:_____

    _____

13. If pictograms are used for permanent signs, is the visual equivalent placed directly below the pictogram?

    _Comments:_____

    _____

14. Are the characters and backgrounds of permanent signs constructed with a matte, nonglare, eggshell colored, or some other nonglare finish?

    _Comments:_____

    _____

N. Controls and Operating Mechanisms

1. Is there clear floor space to approach controls: forward approach, 30 inches wide and 48 inches deep; parallel approach, 48 inches wide and 30 inches deep?

    _Comments:_____

    _____

2. Is the maximum height of light switches and dispensers 48 inches from the floor?

    _Comments:_____

    _____

	YES	NO	N/A

3. Are wall-mounted electrical and communication system receptacles placed no less than 15 inches above the floor? ____ ____ ____

Comments:_____

_____

O. Telephones

1. Are public telephones placed at accessible heights (44 inches) for wheelchair users? ____ ____ ____

Comments:_____

_____

2. Are public telephones identified by the international symbol of accessibility? ____ ____ ____

Comments:_____

_____

3. Are accessible pay telephones located on an accessible route with minimum clear floor space of 30 inches? ____ ____ ____

Comments:_____

_____

4. Is the highest operable part of the accessible pay telephone 48 inches above the floor for front approach or 54 inches above the floor for a parallel approach? ____ ____ ____

Comments:_____

_____

5. Is there a public telephone capable of providing increased volume for the hearing impaired? ____ ____ ____

Comments:_____

_____

6. Are the telephones hearing-aid compatible? ____ ____ ____

Comments:_____

_____

7. Are the telephones touch-tone? ____ ____ ____

Comments:_____

_____

	YES	NO	N/A

8. Is the telephone cord from the telephone to the hand
set at least 29 inches long?

    *Comments:*_____

_____

9. Is a public pay text telephone (TDD; telecommunications device for the deaf) available?

    *Comments:*_____

_____

10. If an acoustic coupler is used, is the telephone cord
long enough to connect the text telephone and the
telephone receiver?

    *Comments:*_____

_____

11. Is signage displaying the international TDD
symbol on the text telephone?

    *Comments:*_____

_____

12. Are telephone books available within reach of
wheelchair users?

    *Comments:*_____

_____

P. Card Catalogs and Magazine Displays

1. Do catalogs/terminals and magazine displays have a
clear minimum aisle space of 36 inches?

    *Comments:*_____

_____

2. Are catalogs/terminals at a 27.5-inch clear minimum
height for wheelchair use?

    *Comments:*_____

_____

3. Is the maximum height of catalogs/terminals and
magazine displays 48 inches?

    *Comments:*_____

_____

	YES	NO	N/A

Q. Book Stacks

1. Is the space between stacks at least 36 to 42 inches
    wide to allow for passage of a wheelchair?

    _Comments:_____

    _____

2. Do stacks have a clear space of 36 inches to 48 inches
    at the ends so a wheelchair can turn corners around
    the stacks? (The clear minimum required is 36 inches,
    but ADA guidelines recommend 42 to 48 inches end
    and cross aisle widths.)

    _Comments:_____

    _____

R. Reading, Study, Bibliographic, and Service Areas

1. Is at least 5 percent, or a minimum of 1 of each
    element, of fixed seating, tables, or study carrels
    accessible?

    _Comments:_____

    _____

2. Is there a clear passage of 36 inches continuous and
    32 inches at a point between tables, chairs, or stacks?

    _Comments:_____

    _____

3. Are there areas of clear space of 60 inches in breadth
    where 180-degree turns may be made?

    _Comments:_____

    _____

4. Is the knee clearance at accessible tables at least 27
    inches high, 30 inches wide, and 19 inches deep?

    _Comments:_____

    _____

5. Are the tops of accessible tables at least 34 inches
    above the floor?

    _Comments:_____

    _____

	YES	NO	N/A

6. If the primary service counters exceed 36 inches in height, is an auxiliary counter provided with a height 28 to 34 inches from the floor? ____ ____ ____

   *Comments:*_____

   _____

7. Are Braille maps available for the blind? ____ ____ ____

   *Comments:*_____

   _____

8. Are Braille brochures available? ____ ____ ____

   *Comments:*_____

   _____

S. Meeting Rooms

1. Does wheelchair seating have a clear view of the stage or front area? ____ ____ ____

   *Comments:*_____

   _____

2. Is companion seating available in the wheelchair area? ____ ____ ____

   *Comments:*_____

   _____

3. Does the meeting room have the correct number of wheelchair locations for seating? ____ ____ ____

Seating Capacity	Required No. of Wheelchair Seats
4 to 25	1
26 to 50	2
51 to 300	4
301 to 500	6
Over 500	6 + 1 additional space for each seating capacity increase over 100

   *Comments:*_____

   _____

4. Does the wheelchair seating adjoin an accessible route which may also serve as a means of egress in case of emergency? ____ ____ ____

	YES	NO	N/A

Comments:_____

_____

5. If the meeting room has flexible seating, are the tables used for wheelchairs accessible with knee space of 27 inches high, 20 inches wide, and 19 inches deep, with the tabletops 28 to 34 inches above the floor?　　____　____　____

Comments:_____

_____

6. Does the meeting room provide an assistive listening system to augment standard public address and audio systems?　　____　____　____

Comments:_____

_____

7. If the meeting room has fixed seating, is the assistive listening system located within a 50-foot viewing distance of the stage or front area?　　____　____　____

Comments:_____

_____

8. Does the signage include the international symbol of access for the hearing impaired to notify patrons of the availability of a listening system?　　____　____　____

Comments:_____

_____

T. Building Facilities

1. Is there a designated Rescue Assistance Area in the facility?　　____　____　____

Comments:_____

_____

2. Are there designated emergency routes in the facility?　　____　____　____

Comments:_____

_____

3. Are these routes easily identified?　　____　____　____

Comments:_____

_____

	YES	NO	N/A
4. Are there signs to guide users in case of emergency?	____	____	____
Comments:_____			
5. Are the signs illuminated?	____	____	____
Comments:_____			
6. Do these signs point the way to the Rescue Assistance Area?	____	____	____
Comments:_____			
7. Is the Rescue Assistance Area enclosed, smoke-proof, and vented to the outside?	____	____	____
Comments:_____			
8. Is the Rescue Assistance Area separated from the building interior by at least 1 fire-resistant door?	____	____	____
Comments:_____			
9. Does the Rescue Assistance Area provide at least 2 accessible 30-by-48-inch wheelchair spaces which do not encroach on the width of any required exit route?	____	____	____
Comments:_____			
10. Is there a two-way communication system between the primary entrance and the Rescue Assistance Area?	____	____	____
Comments:_____			

6 Telecommunications, Electrical, and Miscellaneous Equipment

	YES	NO	N/A

A. General Considerations

1. Is electronic and/or electric equipment in use in the following areas:

   a) Circulation desk? _____ _____ _____

   b) Reference areas? _____ _____ _____

   c) Public areas? _____ _____ _____

   d) Technical areas? _____ _____ _____

   e) Administrative areas? _____ _____ _____

   f) Workrooms? _____ _____ _____

   g) Study rooms? _____ _____ _____

   h) Computer labs? _____ _____ _____

   *Comments:*_____

2. Are workstations staggered to enhance noise control and privacy? _____ _____ _____

   *Comments:*_____

	YES	NO	N/A

3. Has equipment been selected with quiet operation in mind?

Comments:_____

B. Telecommunications Entrances and Closets

1. Is the building entrance facility (the point at which outside cabling interfaces with the interior building backbone cabling) a locked, dedicated, and enclosed room with a plywood termination field provided on two walls? (The plywood should be 3/4 inch, with dimensions of 8 feet high x 39 inches wide.)

   Comments:_____

2. Is there an equipment room (essentially a large telecommunications closet) that houses the main distribution frame, PBXs, secondary voltage protection, etc.? The equipment room is often appended to the entrance facilities or a computer room to allow shared air conditioning, security, fire control, lighting, and limited access.

   Comments:_____

3. Is the room at least 150 square feet of floor space? The rule of thumb is to provide 0.75 square feet of equipment room floor space for every 100 square feet of user workstation area.

   Comments:_____

4. Is the room located away from sources of electro-magnetic interference (transformers, motors, induction heaters, theft detection systems, etc.) until interference is less than 3V/m (volt per meter-unit of electrical strength) across the frequency spectrum?

   Comments:_____

5. Is the room in an area that is not subject to floods?

	YES	NO	N/A

Comments:_____

6. Are all surfaces treated to reduce dust, and walls and ceilings painted white or pastel to improve visibility? ___ ___ ___

Comments:_____

7. Are there single or double (36 inches x 80 inches) lockable doors in order to limit access to the room? ___ ___ ___

Comments:_____

8. Has piping, ductwork, mechanical equipment, power cabling, and unrelated storage been kept out of the equipment room? ___ ___ ___

Comments:_____

9. Is the room maintained 24/hrs./day, 365 days/year, at a temperature of 64 degrees to 75 degrees F, 30 percent to 55 percent humidity, with positive pressure? ___ ___ ___

Comments:_____

10. Is there a minimum of two dedicated 15A, 100 VAC duplex outlets on separate circuits? ___ ___ ___

Comments:_____

11. Are there convenience duplex outlets placed at 6-foot intervals around the perimeter of the room? ___ ___ ___

Comments:_____

12. Has an emergency power system been considered? ___ ___ ___

Comments:_____

13. If the equipment room is more than 300 feet to a service point, have additional telecommunications closets been included? (Recommended size, 10 feet x 11 feet for each 10,000-square-foot area served.) ___ ___ ___

Comments:_____

	YES	NO	N/A
14. Is there a twenty-four-hour security system installed?	____	____	____

Comments:_____

_____

15. Is there a separate fire suppression system?   ____   ____   ____

Comments:_____

_____

C. Horizontal Pathways

Horizontal pathways extend between the telecommunications closet and the work area. A variety of generic pathway options is available. Have the following horizontal pathways been considered? (Options are dependent on the design of the building.)

1. Cable bundles running from the telecom closet along j-hooks suspended above a plenum ceiling, fanning out once a work zone is reached, dropping through interior walls or support columns or raceways, and terminating at an information outlet (I/O)?   ____   ____   ____

Comments:_____

_____

2. Under-floor duct? (Single or dual-level rectangular ducts embedded in greater than 2.5-inch thick concrete flooring.)   ____   ____   ____

Comments:_____

_____

3. Flush duct? (Single-level rectangular duct embedded flush in greater than 1-inch thick concrete flooring.)   ____   ____   ____

Comments:_____

_____

4. Multi-channel raceway? (Cellular raceway ducts capable of routing telecom and power cabling separately in greater than 3-inch thick reinforced concrete.)   ____   ____   ____

Comments:_____

_____

5. Cellular floor? (Preformed hollows, or steel lined cellar, are provided in concrete, with header ducts

	YES	NO	N/A

from the telecom closet arranged at right angles to
the cells.)

*Comments:*_____

6. Trench duct? (A wide, solid tray, sometimes divided
into compartments and fitted with a flat top with
gaskets along its entire length, is embedded flush
with the concrete finish.)

*Comments:*_____

7. Access floor? (Modular floor panels supported by
pedestals, are used in computer rooms and equipment rooms.)

*Comments:*_____

8. Conduit? (Is only used when outlet locations are
permanent, device density low, and flexibility for
future changes is not required.)

*Comments:*_____

9. Perimeter pathways? (This option includes surface,
recessed, molding, and multi-channel raceways.)

*Comments:*_____

D. Cabling and Outlets

1. Is a star topology structured cabling system used?
In a star topology, each work-area telecommunications
outlet is connected to a cross-connect in a telecommunications closet. All cables from a floor or area in the
building therefore run back to one central point for
administration. Each telecommunication closet must be
star wired back to the equipment room for the building.

*Comments:*_____

	YES	NO	N/A

2. Is the structured cabling system compatible with
   the type of media to be used?

   Comments: _____

   _____

3. Based on the media to be transmitted, what cable
   alternatives have been selected:

   a) Unshielded twisted pair (UTP)—4-pair, 24-gauge,
      100 ohm copper cable? (Unshielded twisted pair
      cables closely resemble telephone cables but are
      enhanced for data communications to allow higher
      frequency transmissions. Category 5 cables and
      connection hardware are the minimum usually
      required. They are rated up to 100 MHz and are
      designed to handle any current copper-based
      application for voice, video, or data.)

   b) Shielded twisted pair (STP-A)—2-pair, 22-gauge,
      150 ohm copper cable? (Shielded twisted pair
      systems provide high performance as a result of
      shielding. If used, Category 5 is required.)

   c) Single-mode and multi-mode optical fiber cables?
      (The highest performing structured cabling systems
      use fiber optics, and will be the choice of most
      libraries in the long run.)

   Comments: _____

   _____

4. Does each workstation have a minimum of two
   information outlet ports?

   Comments: _____

   _____

5. Is every seat in the library considered as a workstation
   and equipped with telecommunications outlets? (One
   outlet port is required for voice and the other for data.)

   Comments: _____

   _____

6. Has a wireless system been considered?

   Comments: _____

   _____

	YES	NO	N/A

E. Electrical Power

1. Is there sufficient power distribution throughout the entire facility?

   *Comments:*_____

2. Is it "clean power," with high quality, and reliable?

   *Comments:*_____

3. Is there a backup power system in place?

   *Comments:*_____

4. Does the system provide for future needs?

   *Comments:*_____

5. Is all wiring easily accessible (raised floors, flat wire, grids under carpet, conduits above dropped ceilings or in columns)?

   *Comments:*_____

6. Is surge protection available where needed?

   *Comments:*_____

7. Is voltage regulated at the building feed?

   *Comments:*_____

8. Is voltage regulated at each floor box?

   *Comments:*_____

9. Are dedicated lines available for equipment that requires them (terminals, photocopiers, etc.)?

   *Comments:*_____

10. Are cords and cables protected and out of sight?

    *Comments:*_____

	YES	NO	N/A

11. Does each staff workstation have three to five duplex outlets?

    *Comments:*_____

12. Are there outlets at frequent intervals throughout the building?

    *Comments:*_____

13. Do outlets have electrical and data/telephone capabilities?

    *Comments:*_____

14. Are there specialized wiring arrangements (e.g., wall-mounted power strips or ceiling outlets) for areas such as teleconference, automated demonstration, and computing rooms?

    *Comments:*_____

15. Are floor outlets flush with the surface?

    *Comments:*_____

16. Are public workstations/carrels provided with power and data ports?

    *Comments:*_____

17. Is there a user fee for using the library's power?

    *Comments:*_____

F. Workstation Equipment

1. Are there online public access catalogs (OPAC stations)?

   *Comments:*_____

2. Are there Internet terminals?

   *Comments:*_____

	YES	NO	N/A
3. Are there CD-ROM terminals?	⎯⎯	⎯⎯	⎯⎯
Comments:			

4. Do all terminals provide:

	YES	NO	N/A
a) Hidden wiring?	⎯⎯	⎯⎯	⎯⎯
b) All necessary connection outlets?	⎯⎯	⎯⎯	⎯⎯
c) Adequate work space?	⎯⎯	⎯⎯	⎯⎯
d) Space for printers and paper?	⎯⎯	⎯⎯	⎯⎯
e) Back panels to hide connections and wires from customers?	⎯⎯	⎯⎯	⎯⎯
Comments:			

	YES	NO	N/A
5. Are there printers for all terminals that need them?	⎯⎯	⎯⎯	⎯⎯
Comments:			
6. Are impact printers acoustically controlled?	⎯⎯	⎯⎯	⎯⎯
Comments:			
7. Do public areas have quiet printers (thermal, laser, or ink-jet)?	⎯⎯	⎯⎯	⎯⎯
Comments:			
8. Are microcomputers available to the public for word processing, spreadsheets, and other applications?	⎯⎯	⎯⎯	⎯⎯
Comments:			
9. Is the appropriate software installed to support the above applications?	⎯⎯	⎯⎯	⎯⎯
Comments:			
10. Is there high speed Internet access?	⎯⎯	⎯⎯	⎯⎯
Comments:			

	YES	NO	N/A

G. Telephone System

1. Is there a central telephone system?   ___ ___ ___
   *Comments:*_____

   _____

2. Does it provide for:

   a) Automated attendant?   ___ ___ ___

   b) Voice mail?   ___ ___ ___

   c) Call forwarding?   ___ ___ ___

   d) Teleconferencing (audio or audio/video)?   ___ ___ ___

   e) Automatic redial?   ___ ___ ___

   f) Remote access?   ___ ___ ___

   g) Direct inward dialing?   ___ ___ ___

   h) Toll restriction?   ___ ___ ___

   i) Trunk call queuing?   ___ ___ ___

   j) Paging?   ___ ___ ___

   k) WATS line?   ___ ___ ___

   l) Data transmission?   ___ ___ ___

   m) LAN connection?   ___ ___ ___

   n) Maintenance contract?   ___ ___ ___

   o) Future expansion capabilities?   ___ ___ ___

   *Comments:*_____

   _____

3. Is a switchboard operator required?   ___ ___ ___
   *Comments:*_____

   _____

4. If so, is there adequate space for operators to do other
   work when not answering the phone?   ___ ___ ___
   *Comments:*_____

   _____

	YES	NO	N/A

5. Are alternative long-distance vendors used? ____ ____ ____

   *Comments:*_____

   _____

6. Are telephones hard-wired? ____ ____ ____

   *Comments:*_____

   _____

7. Are incoming lines sufficient in number and quality? ____ ____ ____

   *Comments:*_____

   _____

8. Are there dedicated spare lines for modem access? ____ ____ ____

   *Comments:*_____

   _____

9. Are public telephones located to allow for convenient
   use while preventing disturbance to other customers? ____ ____ ____

   *Comments:*_____

   _____

10. Are the public telephones set up for outgoing calls only? ____ ____ ____

    *Comments:*_____

    _____

11. Are telephone directories provided? ____ ____ ____

    *Comments:*_____

    _____

12. Are coin-changing machines available near the
    telephones? ____ ____ ____

    *Comments:*_____

    _____

13. Are there cordless telephones for staff use? ____ ____ ____

    *Comments:*_____

    _____

14. Is the library involved in a network with branches
    and/or other libraries via telecommunications and
    data transfer? ____ ____ ____

    *Comments:*_____

    _____

	YES	NO	N/A

H. Miscellaneous Electrical Equipment

1. Are standard television sets in use? ____ ____ ____
   *Comments:*_____

   _____

2. Are the television sets staff controlled? ____ ____ ____
   *Comments:*_____

   _____

3. Are television sets with decoders for digital data
   available? ____ ____ ____
   *Comments:*_____

   _____

4. Is there provision for large-screen television viewing
   in meeting or conference rooms? ____ ____ ____
   *Comments:*_____

   _____

5. Is there access to cable TV? ____ ____ ____
   *Comments:*_____

   _____

6. Is there a satellite uplink? ____ ____ ____
   *Comments:*_____

   _____

7. Is there a satellite downlink? ____ ____ ____
   *Comments:*_____

   _____

8. Is packet radio in use and is provision adequate? ____ ____ ____
   *Comments:*_____

   _____

9. Are video recorder/players available for public use? ____ ____ ____
   *Comments:*_____

   _____

10. Are there teleconferencing and distance learning facilities? ____ ____ ____
    *Comments:*_____

    _____

	YES	NO	N/A
11. Is microwave transmission/reception used?	____	____	____
Comments:_____			
_____			
12. Is there a public-address system?	____	____	____
Comments:_____			
_____			

Interior Design and Finishes

	YES	NO	N/A

A. Service Desks

1. Whom does the service desk serve? Adults, children, students?   ____ ____ ____

   Comments: _____

   _____

2. What type of service desks are required:

   a) Control or security desk?   ____ ____ ____

   b) Directional or information desk?   ____ ____ ____

   c) Circulation or charge desk?   ____ ____ ____

   d) Call or delivery desk?   ____ ____ ____

   e) Reference desk?   ____ ____ ____

   f) Reference consultation center?   ____ ____ ____

   Comments: _____

   _____

3. Is the design of the desk area flexible, allowing possible future relocation, new technology, or even elimination of the desk?   ____ ____ ____

   Comments: _____

   _____

	YES	NO	N/A

4. What kind of way finding system and signs lead people to the service desks? ____ ____ ____

   *Comments:*_____

   _____

5. Is the desk located in a visible location so that it is obvious to people who need the services provided at the desk? ____ ____ ____

   *Comments:*_____

   _____

6. Is the desk sized to accommodate all staff working at the desk, as well as their storage requirements? ____ ____ ____

   *Comments:*_____

   _____

7. Is the desk and surrounding work space designed to be ergonomically correct for staff and customers? ____ ____ ____

   *Comments:*_____

   _____

8. Have customer self-service features been factored into the desk, such as self-check, electronic registration, etc.? ____ ____ ____

   *Comments:*_____

   _____

9. Can conversations at the desk be conducted with a sense of privacy? ____ ____ ____

   *Comments:*_____

   _____

10. How has noise from the service desk from conversations, equipment, phones, etc., been addressed so that nearby spaces are not disrupted? ____ ____ ____

    *Comments:*_____

    _____

11. Have openness and accessibility been maintained while protecting staff from potential aggressive users? ____ ____ ____

    *Comments:*_____

    _____

	YES	NO	N/A

12. Are grommets, wire channels, and equipment shielding provided to present a clean appearance?

    *Comments:*_____

    _____

13. Have sufficient electrical outlets, data and telephone ports been provided?

    *Comments:*_____

    _____

14. Is the desk protected from drafts or other changing environmental conditions?

    *Comments:*_____

    _____

15. Are the desk finishes and materials highly durable?

    *Comments:*_____

    _____

16. Can the desk surfaces and edges be easily cleaned?

    *Comments:*_____

    _____

B. Seating

1. Is there variety in the types of seating?

    *Comments:*_____

    _____

2. Is lounge seating modular or heavy enough to discourage casual rearrangement by customers, unless the library desires rearrangement?

    *Comments:*_____

    _____

3. Is adequate and appropriate seating provided for varying tasks and areas:

    a) Staff work areas?

    b) Public seating at tables and carrels?

    c) Lounge areas?

	YES	NO	N/A

d) Reference areas? ____ ____ ____

e) Meeting rooms? ____ ____ ____

*Comments:*_____

4. Is seating appropriate for different ages? ____ ____ ____
*Comments:*_____

5. Are people (especially senior citizens) able to get in and out of chairs easily? ____ ____ ____
*Comments:*_____

6. Is seating comfortable for those areas where the library wants users to relax and read for an extended period? ____ ____ ____
*Comments:*_____

7. Is seating comfortable but conducive to quick turnover for those areas where you want users to leave after their work task is completed? (The two types of seating can be exemplified by the seating available in a fast-food restaurant versus that found in a fine restaurant.) ____ ____ ____
*Comments:*_____

8. Are chairs ergonomically correct? ____ ____ ____
*Comments:*_____

9. Is seating attractive and inviting? ____ ____ ____
*Comments:*_____

10. Is furniture free of projections that could snag clothing? ____ ____ ____
*Comments:*_____

11. Is furniture relatively free from sharp corners? ____ ____ ____
*Comments:*_____

	YES	NO	N/A

12. Does seating take personal space into consideration to avoid psychological feelings of crowding? ___ ___ ___

Comments: _____

_____

13. If the chair has arms, will the arms fit comfortably under work surfaces? ___ ___ ___

Comments: _____

_____

14. Are footstools or ottomans provided? ___ ___ ___

Comments: _____

_____

15. Is furniture designed for easy repair or replacement of parts? ___ ___ ___

Comments: _____

_____

16. Is furniture constructed for user safety? ___ ___ ___

Comments: _____

_____

17. Has the furniture been used successfully in similar library or other public situations for several years? ___ ___ ___

Comments: _____

_____

18. Are performance data available to attest to the durability of the chair? ___ ___ ___

Comments: _____

_____

19. Has seating been stress tested? ___ ___ ___

Comments: _____

_____

20. Do chairs with casters move easily on carpet? ___ ___ ___

Comments: _____

_____

21. Is lounge seating modular or heavy enough not to tip over? ___ ___ ___

Comments: _____

_____

	YES	NO	N/A

22. Are fabrics sturdy and soil resistant?

    *Comments:*_____

    _____

23. Do the chair design and the kind of upholstery or
    finish used allow for easy cleaning?

    *Comments:*_____

    _____

24. Can the chair be easily reupholstered or refinished?

    *Comments:*_____

    _____

25. Is the fabric porous enough to "breathe" and able to
    absorb and evaporate moisture easily?

    *Comments:*_____

    _____

26. Do lounge chairs with upholstered arms have arm
    covers to preserve appearance?

    *Comments:*_____

    _____

27. Are chairs designed so that the area under the chair
    can be easily reached by a vacuum cleaner?

    *Comments:*_____

    _____

28. Does the supplier warranty the design and construc-
    tion of the seats?

    *Comments:*_____

    _____

C. Tables

1. Are the tables appropriate for the task intended?

   *Comments:*_____

   _____

2. Are the tables durable and strong?

   *Comments:*_____

   _____

	YES	NO	N/A

3. Is the work surface material appropriate for the use anticipated?   ___   ___   ___

Comments:_____

_____

4. Can the work surface be easily maintained?   ___   ___   ___

Comments:_____

_____

5. Can the work surface be easily refinished?   ___   ___   ___

Comments:_____

_____

6. Does the table have any needed accessories, such as task lighting, electrical outlets, etc.?   ___   ___   ___

Comments:_____

_____

7. Is there a mixture of circular tables (for socializing) and rectangular tables (better for work and concentration) on the floor?   ___   ___   ___

Comments:_____

_____

8. Are there enough carrels for individual studying?   ___   ___   ___

Comments:_____

_____

9. Does the supplier warranty the design and construction of the table?   ___   ___   ___

Comments:_____

_____

10. What is the length of the warranty?   ___   ___   ___

Comments:_____

_____

D. Lighting

1. Is the intensity of the general lighting sufficient for reading?   ___   ___   ___

Comments:_____

_____

	YES	NO	N/A

2. Is the "task lighting" adequate for carrels, work stations, separate desks, lounge furniture, and shelving areas?

    *Comments:*_____

_____

3. In addition to general and task lighting, do certain areas of the library have special lighting? For example, do wall display areas have track lighting?

    *Comments:*_____

_____

4. Is lighting adequate at the lower shelf areas in book stacks? (Lighting levels drop dramatically from the top to the bottom of book stacks.)

    *Comments:*_____

_____

5. Are light switches conveniently located?

    *Comments:*_____

_____

6. Can library staff control the switching of lights from a central control point or points?

    *Comments:*_____

_____

7. Is the lighting control sytem designed so that customers can't switch lights on and off in those areas where public control is not desirable?

    *Comments:*_____

_____

E. Windows

1. Has the library considered the trade-off between the positive aspects of windows (natural light, fresh air, and pleasant vistas) vs. the negative factors (the possible waste of energy, the loss of outside walls as book-stack areas, and the impact of uncontrolled sunlight on materials and readers)?

    *Comments:*_____

_____

	YES	NO	N/A

2. Are some of the windows placed close to the ceiling
to allow a higher intensity of light? ____ ____ ____
   *Comments:*_____
   _____

3. Are some of the windows placed at eye level, especially
in reading areas and in areas occupied by the staff for
positive psychological effect? ____ ____ ____
   *Comments:*_____
   _____

4. Can windows be shaded on demand to prevent light
from interfering with reading and other activities? ____ ____ ____
   *Comments:*_____
   _____

5. Are books stored away from direct sunlight to protect
the bindings from fading and to prevent paper
deterioration? ____ ____ ____
   *Comments:*_____
   _____

6. If the regional climate suggests it, are windows double-
glazed to allow for enhanced energy efficiency? ____ ____ ____
   *Comments:*_____
   _____

7. If the regional climate allows it, are windows operable
to allow for natural cooling and ventilation? ____ ____ ____
   *Comments:*_____
   _____

8. Are a limited number of windows operable to allow
for maintenance and emergency situations? ____ ____ ____
   *Comments:*_____
   _____

9. If windows can be opened, are they securable by the
staff from the inside? ____ ____ ____
   *Comments:*_____
   _____

	YES	NO	N/A

F. Flooring

1. Has the trade-off between types of floor coverings been considered by examining the:

   a) Original construction costs? ⸻ ⸻ ⸻

   b) Total useful life of the floor covering? ⸻ ⸻ ⸻

   c) Appropriateness of the floor covering for the area to be covered? ⸻ ⸻ ⸻

   d) Ease of maintenance? ⸻ ⸻ ⸻

   e) Cost of maintenance? ⸻ ⸻ ⸻

   f) Ease of replacement? ⸻ ⸻ ⸻

   g) Cost of replacement? ⸻ ⸻ ⸻

   *Comments:*_____

   _____

2. Are special floor-covering materials or systems used at the entry and places of heavy traffic to prevent dirt, mud, slush, and water from being tracked onto the carpet? ⸻ ⸻ ⸻
   *Comments:*_____

   _____

3. Have carpet tiles or squares been considered for easy access to under-floor power systems as well as ease of replacement when damaged or soiled? ⸻ ⸻ ⸻
   *Comments:*_____

   _____

4. Is the carpet of first-class quality to ensure durability? ⸻ ⸻ ⸻
   *Comments:*_____

   _____

5. Does the carpet color conceal soiling and resist fading? ⸻ ⸻ ⸻
   *Comments:*_____

   _____

6. Does flooring minimize noise and enhance building acoustics? ⸻ ⸻ ⸻
   *Comments:*_____

   _____

	YES	NO	N/A

7. Can book trucks be moved easily across the flooring? _____ _____ _____

Comments: _____

_____

8. Is ceramic tile or a similar material used on the rest-room floors for its sanitary appearance and ease of maintenance? _____ _____ _____

Comments: _____

_____

9. If pavement tiles (stone, marble, or granite) are used in entryways and lobbies, are provisions made for safety since these become very slippery when wet? _____ _____ _____

Comments: _____

_____

10. Has concrete flooring, if left uncovered, been treated with a filler and then painted to prevent dust from becoming troublesome? _____ _____ _____

Comments: _____

_____

11. If wood floors are used, does the library's operating budget allow for the care needed to keep them in good condition? _____ _____ _____

Comments: _____

_____

G. Walls

1. Have "wet" interior walls been avoided as much as possible? (Wet walls are those that cannot be removed without demolishing them.) _____ _____ _____

Comments: _____

_____

2. Are the wall coverings and surfaces appropriate for the room's function? _____ _____ _____

Comments: _____

_____

3. Will the care and selection of wall coverings result in years of added wear and minimum upkeep? _____ _____ _____

	YES	NO	N/A

Comments:_____

_____

4. Are areas subject to soiling covered with a washable
paint with a glossy finish?   ____   ____   ____
Comments:_____

_____

5. Is matte or dull finish used where reflectivity is a
concern?   ____   ____   ____
Comments:_____

_____

6. To add interest, are there special wall treatments such
as stenciling, textured materials such as a woven fabric,
or wood paneling?   ____   ____   ____
Comments:_____

_____

7. Have other materials such as brick and stone been
used for wall coverings?   ____   ____   ____
Comments:_____

_____

8. Is ceramic tile used for the walls in the rest rooms for
ease of maintenance?   ____   ____   ____
Comments:_____

_____

9. If ceramic tile has been used to create decorative wall
murals, has care been taken to minimize the acoustical
impact of the hard surface?   ____   ____   ____
Comments:_____

_____

10. Have vinyl wall coverings been considered for areas
of heavy use, including hallways and staircases?   ____   ____   ____
Comments:_____

_____

11. Have vinyl wall coverings with special sound-absorbing
properties been considered for offices, workrooms,
and conference rooms?   ____   ____   ____
Comments:_____

_____

	YES	NO	N/A

12. Do the walls have tackboard surfaces so that they may be used for occasional displays? _____ _____ _____

*Comments:*_____

_____

H. Color

1. Have colors that may quickly become outdated been avoided? _____ _____ _____

   *Comments:*_____

   _____

2. Has particular attention been given to the psychological effects of color on both users and staff? _____ _____ _____

   *Comments:*_____

   _____

3. Has color been considered with respect to the function of the area? _____ _____ _____

   *Comments:*_____

   _____

4. Has color been used to avoid an institutional (drab) aspect with respect to walls, book stacks, floors, and furniture? _____ _____ _____

   *Comments:*_____

   _____

5. Do book stacks on different floors or areas utilize different colors for easy identification? _____ _____ _____

   *Comments:*_____

   _____

6. Have standard paint colors (not mixed) been supplied by the manufacturer for easy, cost-effective maintenance and touch-ups? _____ _____ _____

   *Comments:*_____

   _____

7. Will the upholstery colors selected disguise heavy and sometimes abusive use? _____ _____ _____

   *Comments:*_____

   _____

	YES	NO	N/A

8. Has the relationship of wall, furniture, and floor colors to the lighting of the various areas been considered? ____ ____ ____

Comments: _____

_____

I. Equipment List

Is the following equipment planned for use in the library? If so, is there adequate space, wiring, furniture, and staff available to support it?

	YES	NO	N/A		YES	NO	N/A

1. Catalog terminals? ____ ____ ____

   Comments: _____

   _____

   _____

6. LAN system? ____ ____ ____

   Comments: _____

   _____

2. Microcomputers? ____ ____ ____

   Comments: _____

   _____

   _____

7. Staff telephones with hold and transfer capabilities? ____ ____ ____

   Comments: _____

   _____

3. Computer printers? ____ ____ ____

   Comments: _____

   _____

   _____

8. Public telephones? ____ ____ ____

   Comments: _____

   _____

   _____

4. Modems? ____ ____ ____

   Comments: _____

   _____

   _____

9. Cordless telephones? ____ ____ ____

   Comments: _____

5. CD-ROM (drives, towers, jukeboxes)? ____ ____ ____

   Comments: _____

   _____

   _____

	YES	NO	N/A

10. Mobile two-way com-
munication system? ____ ____ ____
Comments: _____
____. _____
_____
_____

11. Answering machines
or voice mail? ____ ____ ____
Comments: _____
_____
_____
_____

12. Staff paging beepers? ____ ____ ____
Comments: _____
_____
_____
_____

13. Public address system? ____ ____ ____
Comments: _____
_____
_____
_____

14. Telefacsimile (fax)
machines? ____ ____ ____
Comments: _____
_____
_____
_____

15. Voice-synthesis read-
ing machines? ____ ____ ____
Comments: _____
_____
_____
_____

16. Public text telephones
(TDDs)? ____ ____ ____
Comments: _____
_____
_____
_____

17. Electric typewriters? ____ ____ ____
Comments: _____
_____
_____
_____

18. Large-print type-
writers? ____ ____ ____
Comments: _____
_____
_____
_____

19. Word processors? ____ ____ ____
Comments: _____
_____
_____
_____

20. Audio recorders/
players? ____ ____ ____
Comments: _____
_____
_____
_____

21. Video recorders/
players? ____ ____ ____
Comments: _____
_____
_____
_____

22. Tape duplicators? ____ ____ ____
Comments: _____
_____
_____
_____

23. Video disc players? ____ ____ ____
Comments: _____
_____
_____

	YES	**NO**	**N/A**

24. Compact disc players?____ ____ ____
    Comments: _____
    _____
    _____
    _____

25. Record players?   ____ ____ ____
    Comments: _____
    _____
    _____
    _____

26. Headphones?   ____ ____ ____
    Comments: _____
    _____
    _____
    _____

27. Film projectors and screens?   ____ ____ ____
    Comments: _____
    _____
    _____
    _____

28. Video projectors?   ____ ____ ____
    Comments: _____
    _____
    _____
    _____

29. Slide projectors?   ____ ____ ____
    Comments: _____
    _____
    _____
    _____

30. Light table (for slides and/or tracing maps)?   ____ ____ ____
    Comments: _____
    _____
    _____
    _____

31. Overhead projectors?____ ____ ____
    Comments: _____

	YES	**NO**	**N/A**

_____
_____
_____

32. Microform readers?   ____ ____ ____
    Comments: _____
    _____
    _____
    _____

33. Microform readers/ printers?   ____ ____ ____
    Comments: _____
    _____
    _____
    _____

34. Photocopiers?   ____ ____ ____
    Comments: _____
    _____
    _____
    _____

35. Card-operated photo-copiers?   ____ ____ ____
    Comments: _____
    _____
    _____
    _____

36. Clocks strategically located and visible in all public places, as well as easily acces-sible or centrally controlled?   ____ ____ ____
    Comments: _____
    _____
    _____
    _____

37. Time clocks?   ____ ____ ____
    Comments: _____
    _____
    _____
    _____

	YES	NO	N/A

38. Fire hoses? ____ ____ ____

Comments: _____
_____
_____
_____

39. Fire extinguishers? ____ ____ ____

Comments: _____
_____
_____
_____

40. Emergency lights? ____ ____ ____

Comments: _____
_____
_____
_____

41. Emergency power (generators)? ____ ____ ____

Comments: _____
_____
_____
_____

42. Closed-circuit TV systems? ____ ____ ____

Comments: _____
_____
_____
_____

43. Security mirrors? ____ ____ ____

Comments: _____
_____
_____
_____

44. Emergency call system direct to police or security company? ____ ____ ____

Comments: _____
_____
_____
_____

	YES	NO	N/A

45. Emergency call buttons located at service desks and work-rooms? ____ ____ ____

Comments: _____
_____
_____
_____

46. Book trucks:

a) Are they top quality with solid joints and pivoting wheels? ____ ____ ____

b) Do they roll smoothly and quietly on all floor surfaces? ____ ____ ____

c) Are they equipped with shelf height, depth, and slant to accommodate materials of various sizes? ____ ____ ____

d) Are there suffi-cient quantities of trucks in various sizes and configur-ations? ____ ____ ____

Comments: _____
_____
_____
_____

47. Chalkboards/white boards? ____ ____ ____

Comments: _____
_____
_____
_____

48. Bulletin boards? ____ ____ ____

Comments: _____
_____

	YES	NO	N/A

49. Easels?

    Comments: _____

50. Lecterns?

    Comments: _____

51. Display racks?

    Comments: _____

52. Globes?

    Comments: _____

53. Bookends in appro-
    priate sizes and
    shapes?

    Comments: _____

54. Pencil sharpeners?

    Comments: _____

55. Pencil dispensers?

    Comments: _____

	YES	NO	N/A

56. Filing cabinets?

    Comments: _____

57. Electric staplers?

    Comments: _____

58. Hole punches?

    Comments: _____

59. Paper cutters?

    Comments: _____

60. Board cutter?

    Comments: _____

61. Gang punch?

    Comments: _____

62. Wire stitcher?

    Comments: _____

63. Label-pasting machine?

    Comments: _____

	YES	NO	N/A

64. Standing press? _____ _____ _____

Comments: _____

_____

_____

_____

65. Map edger? _____ _____ _____

Comments: _____

_____

_____

_____

66. Laminating machine?_____ _____ _____

Comments: _____

_____

_____

_____

67. Sign and label
makers? _____ _____ _____

Comments: _____

_____

_____

_____

68. Vacuum cleaners? _____ _____ _____

Comments: _____

_____

_____

_____

69. Cleaning supply
carts? _____ _____ _____

Comments: _____

_____

_____

_____

70. Mops, buckets,
brooms, and dust-
pans? _____ _____ _____

Comments: _____

_____

_____

_____

	YES	NO	N/A

71. Trash compactor? _____ _____ _____

Comments: _____

_____

_____

_____

72. Wastebaskets? _____ _____ _____

Comments: _____

_____

_____

_____

73. Recycling containers?_____ _____ _____

Comments: _____

_____

_____

_____

74. Ladders, short and
tall? _____ _____ _____

Comments: _____

_____

_____

_____

75. Step stools? _____ _____ _____

Comments: _____

_____

_____

_____

76. Moving equip-
ment (dollies, carts)? _____ _____ _____

Comments: _____

_____

_____

_____

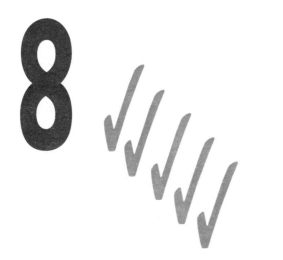

Book Stacks and Shelving

Library Technology Reports, "Test Reports on 15 Models of Bracket-Type Steel Library Bookstacks" (Volume 34, Number 6, November-December 1998), and Library Technology Reports, "Movable Compact Shelving Systems: Selection and Specifications" (Volume 35, Number 5, September-October 1999) are excellent sources for detailed shelving information.

	YES	NO	N/A

A. Conventional Stationary Stacks and Shelving

1. Has sufficient shelving been planned to meet the current and future needs of the library? (Consider size of the current collection, growth of the collection for at least 20 years, and the percentage of the collection that will be out on loan. A rule of thumb for roughly calculating shelving requirements is to assume 150 volumes per 3-foot single-faced section, 7 shelves high.)

   Comments:

2. Is the shelving selection based on the standard titled ANSI/NISO Z239.73 1994, Single-Tier Steel Bracket Library Shelving?

   Comments:

	YES	NO	N/A

3. Are book stacks arranged sequentially in parallel ranges so that users can easily locate materials? ____ ____ ____

   *Comments:*_____

4. If book stacks are not arranged sequentially in parallel ranges, are variations clearly indicated? ____ ____ ____

   *Comments:*_____

5. Are there labels on both ends of ranges? ____ ____ ____

   *Comments:*_____

6. Is display shelving included to merchandise the collection? For example, are there: ____ ____ ____

   a) Display units with sloping shelves? ____ ____ ____

   b) Point-of-purchase displays as seen in bookstores and department stores? ____ ____ ____

   c) Spinners or towers? ____ ____ ____

   d) Slat-wall end panels or wall units? ____ ____ ____

   *Comments:*_____

7. Are all stacks and shelves clearly labeled as to content on both end panels and shelf lips? ____ ____ ____

   *Comments:*_____

8. Are there attempts to break the monotony of shelving by creative arrangement of seating or height and/or type of shelving? ____ ____ ____

   *Comments:*_____

9. Are there no more than eight 36-inch sections without a break? ____ ____ ____

   *Comments:*_____

10. Have length of shelving and width of aisles been determined on the basis of traffic patterns and user accessibility? (See section 5.) ____ ____ ____

	YES	NO	N/A

*Comments:*_____

_____

11. Are the shelving height and depth adequate for uses?   ____   ____   ____

*Comments:*_____

_____

12. Do double-faced sections of bracket shelving have
bases 20 or 40 inches deep?   ____   ____   ____

*Comments:*_____

_____

13. Is freestanding shelving, ranging from 78 inches or
higher, anchored to the floor, or braced with top
tie struts?   ____   ____   ____

*Comments:*_____

_____

14. Are the shelving units:

    a) Sturdy and well built?   ____   ____   ____

    b) Able to bear prescribed loads without sagging,
bending, leaning, swaying, or collapsing?   ____   ____   ____

    c) Equipped with a finish that will endure normal
use and cleaning for at least 30 years without
signs of wear?   ____   ____   ____

    d) Smoothly finished with no burrs or sharp edges?   ____   ____   ____

    e) Standardized in design and color?   ____   ____   ____

    f) Designed to have interchangeable parts?   ____   ____   ____

    g) Equipped with adjustable shelves?   ____   ____   ____

    h) Equipped with shelves that are relatively easy to
move when they are unloaded?   ____   ____   ____

    i) Equipped with shelves that are relatively easy to
move when they are loaded?   ____   ____   ____

    j) Braced and/or anchored to comply with local
regulations?   ____   ____   ____

    k) Equipped with end panels?   ____   ____   ____

    l) Equipped with canopies?   ____   ____   ____

*Comments:*_____

	YES	NO	N/A

15. Are there special features such as:

   a) Pull-out shelves? _____ _____ _____

   b) Built-in lighting? _____ _____ _____

   c) Electrical access? _____ _____ _____

   d) Shelf dividers? _____ _____ _____

   e) Movable book supports of adequate size? _____ _____ _____

   f) Range-label holders? _____ _____ _____

   g) Shelf-label holders? _____ _____ _____

   h) Current periodical shelves? _____ _____ _____

   i) Wide-lip newspaper shelves? _____ _____ _____

   j) Atlas and dictionary stands? _____ _____ _____

   *Comments:*_____

16. Are there accessories to display and house: _____ _____ _____

   a) Audiocassettes? _____ _____ _____

   b) Videocassettes? _____ _____ _____

   c) Compact discs? _____ _____ _____

   d) Picture books? _____ _____ _____

   e) Paperback books? _____ _____ _____

   f) Oversized and miniature materials? _____ _____ _____

   g) Archival materials? _____ _____ _____

   h) Films, filmstrips, slides, microforms? _____ _____ _____

   i) Realia? _____ _____ _____

   j) Other odd-shaped items? _____ _____ _____

   *Comments:*_____

17. Does periodical shelving have a maximum reach
height of 48 inches? _____ _____ _____

   *Comments:*_____

	YES	NO	N/A

18. Does periodical shelving have sloping shelves that tilt and allow for storage on a flat shelf beneath?

_Comments:_____

19. Is the edge or lip on newspaper shelves wide enough to hold a large Sunday edition? (Use the Sunday _New York Times_ after Thanksgiving as a test.)

_Comments:_____

20. Is there a need for enclosed shelving with lockable doors?

_Comments:_____

21. Are there shelf/table units for reference and index materials?

_Comments:_____

22. Have nonpublic work and storage areas been provided with appropriate shelving?

_Comments:_____

B. Movable-Aisle Compact Shelving

1. Is the building capable of holding the substantial weight of a compact installation? (Generally, floor load capacity for compact shelving is 300 pounds live load per square foot.)

_Comments:_____

2. Does the cost of the space saved justify the cost of the system?

_Comments:_____

3. Are all ADA and safety codes met?

_Comments:_____

	YES	NO	N/A

4. If the rails cannot be recessed, will there be some kind
   of deck for the system?

   *Comments:*_____

   _____

5. Are the shelving units moved manually or are they
   motorized?

   *Comments:*_____

   _____

6. If an electrical system is used, does it have a manual
   override?

   *Comments:*_____

   _____

7. Is there a "fail-safe system" that stops the movement
   of the units if an obstacle is encountered?

   *Comments:*_____

   _____

8. Have the specialized cleaning and maintenance needs
   of compact shelving been considered?

   *Comments:*_____

   _____

9. Will the vendor install the system?

   *Comments:*_____

   _____

10. Will the vendor maintain the system?

    *Comments:*_____

    _____

11. Will movable stacks be accessible to the public with or
    without staff assistance?

    *Comments:*_____

    _____

12. Can the system be expanded?

    *Comments:*_____

    _____

13. Can the system be moved?

    *Comments:*_____

    _____

	YES	NO	N/A

C. Automatic Retrieval Systems

1. Is a mechanized book-retrieval system needed? ____ ____ ____
    *Comments:*_____

2. Have the following been considered before deciding
    upon a mechanized book-retrieval system:

    a) Size of the collection? ____ ____ ____

    b) Space available for the collection? ____ ____ ____

    c) Growth of the collection? ____ ____ ____

    d) Contingency plans if the system fails? ____ ____ ____

    e) Cost of staffing? ____ ____ ____

    f) Cost of installation and maintenance? ____ ____ ____

    g) Load-bearing capabilities of the building? ____ ____ ____

    *Comments:*_____

9

Building Systems

	YES	NO	N/A

A. HVAC (Heating, Ventilation, and Air Conditioning) System

1. Is the HVAC system:

    a) Simple to operate? ____ ____ ____

    b) Easy to maintain? ____ ____ ____

    c) Efficient to run? ____ ____ ____

    *Comments:*_____

    _____

2. Does the system, including ductwork, make efficient use of space? ____ ____ ____

    *Comments:*_____

    _____

3. Can temperature and humidity be zone-controlled room by room, either centrally or from lockable thermostats? ____ ____ ____

    *Comments:*_____

    _____

4. Is the building properly insulated to help maintain temperature efficiently? ____ ____ ____

    *Comments:*_____

    _____

	YES	NO	N/A

5. If the building has large windows or skylights, is there provision for maintaining temperature through window coverings or special glazing?

    *Comments:*_____

6. Is there adequate ventilation using:

    a) A mechanical air-exchange system?

    b) Natural ventilation?

    *Comments:*_____

7. Is there provision for ventilation if the climate control fails?

    *Comments:*_____

8. Do the windows open?

    *Comments:*_____

9. Can environmental pollution be filtered out of the air?

    *Comments:*_____

10. Can humidity be controlled within a 5 percent variance?

    *Comments:*_____

11. Are temperature/humidity conditions appropriate for:

    a) Rare materials?

    b) Special collections?

    c) Archives?

    d) Computer stations, computer labs, and telecommunication rooms?

    e) Public areas?

    f) Staff work areas?

    g) Closed stacks?

    *Comments:*_____

	YES	NO	N/A

12. Are there emergency backup generators that can be used if the electricity goes off and the air conditioning shuts down?

Comments:_____

B. Lighting

1. Is lighting energy- and cost-efficient?

Comments:_____

2. Can all interior lights be turned on/off from one location?

Comments:_____

3. Can staff operate a light control at staff entrances, allowing adequate illumination before arriving at the main control point for interior lighting?

Comments:_____

4. Is the building's night lighting adequate to allow observation of the library's interior through outside windows?

Comments:_____

5. Is lighting in all areas adequate and glare free?

Comments:_____

6. Are rheostat (dimmer) controls available at individual workstations to permit local adjustment to user need?

Comments:_____

7. Are the following lighting levels maintained (generally based on the 1993 *Lighting Handbook of the Illuminating Engineering Society of North America*):

   a) Reading areas: 30 to 40 foot-candles (300–400 lux) average, measured horizontally at desktop, and augmented with task lighting carrels and at tables where appropriate?

	YES	NO	N/A

b) Stacks: 6 foot-candles (60 lux) minimum measured vertically at a height of 12 inches, and 30 foot candles (300 lux) maximum measured vertically at any height to achieve approximately 5:1 maximum-to-minimum ratio across the entire stack face?

c) Small conference or group study rooms: 30 to 40 foot-candles (300–400 lux) average, measured horizontally at desktop?

d) Staff areas: 50 foot-candles (500 lux) average on desks or work tables measured horizontally at desktop?

e) Large meeting or community rooms: 40 foot-candles (400 lux) average with all lights on, and with separately controlled lighting for the podium or front of the room?

f) Parking lot: 0.6 foot-candles (6 lux) minimum, measured horizontally on pavement, to achieve a 4:1 average-to-minimum ratio, and with no spill light on adjacent properties?

*Comments:*_____

8. Are light switches located where they can be easily and logically accessed, not behind door swings or large pieces of equipment?
*Comments:*_____

9. Are ambient and task lights on timers or motion detectors in closed stacks, offices, and/or public areas?
*Comments:*_____

10. Can ambient lighting be dimmed or brightened according to need?
*Comments:*_____

11. Is lighting zoned so various areas can be dimmed or brightened independently?
*Comments:*_____

	YES	NO	N/A

12. Is flexible, timed programming available for each
    lighting zone?   ___   ___   ___
    *Comments:*_____
    _____

13. Are light zones identified by switch labels?   ___   ___   ___
    *Comments:*_____
    _____

14. Can daylight be used as a source of lighting?   ___   ___   ___
    *Comments:*_____
    _____

15. If daylight is used, can it be controlled by window
    coverings, tinted glass, or other special glazing?   ___   ___   ___
    *Comments:*_____
    _____

16. When natural lighting is used, is it designed to elimi-
    nate glare and "hot spots" of intense light and/or heat?   ___   ___   ___
    *Comments:*_____
    _____

17. Are seasonal light changes taken into account?   ___   ___   ___
    *Comments:*_____
    _____

18. Will ultraviolet light be filtered from fluorescent and
    natural light sources?   ___   ___   ___
    *Comments:*_____
    _____

19. Are computer monitors and other video screens
    shielded from direct sunlight or glare?   ___   ___   ___
    *Comments:*_____
    _____

20. Can lighting be easily moved if furniture, shelving,
    or equipment is moved?   ___   ___   ___
    *Comments:*_____
    _____

21. Is the lighting system easily replaced and maintained?   ___   ___   ___
    *Comments:*_____
    _____

22. Are exterior lighting fixtures of vandal-resistant
    construction?   ___   ___   ___

	YES	NO	N/A

*Comments:*_____

23. Do exterior lighting fixtures have durable finishes
    to protect them from weather?   ____   ____   ____
    *Comments:*_____

24. Has the number of different lamp types been minimized
    to simplify maintenance and lamp stocking?   ____   ____   ____
    *Comments:*_____

25. Are replacement lamps:

    a) Easily accessible?   ____   ____   ____

    b) Reasonably priced?   ____   ____   ____

    *Comments:*_____

C. Noise

1. Are circulation, information, and reference service
   points located and designed so noise will not disrupt
   other areas?   ____   ____   ____
   *Comments:*_____

2. Have rest rooms, conference rooms, lounges, photocopiers, and public telephones been located where
   the noise will be the least distracting?   ____   ____   ____
   *Comments:*_____

3. Are traffic patterns throughout the building designed
   to keep noise and confusion away from readers?   ____   ____   ____
   *Comments:*_____

4. Are there acoustically controlled quiet areas and are
   they accessible from widely distributed entrance points?   ____   ____   ____
   *Comments:*_____

	YES	NO	N/A

5. Are soundproof rooms available?   ___   ___   ___

Comments: _____

_____

6. Is there acoustical separation between public and
staff areas?   ___   ___   ___

Comments: _____

_____

7. Are mechanical systems (elevators, heating, and air
conditioning equipment) located away from quiet
areas and/or acoustically shielded?   ___   ___   ___

Comments: _____

_____

8. Are there areas where furniture is arranged so as to
discourage conversation?   ___   ___   ___

Comments: _____

_____

9. Has equipment in public areas (computer printers,
photocopiers, etc.) been chosen for quiet operation?   ___   ___   ___

Comments: _____

_____

10. Is there background sound, such as the ventilating
system or other "white noise" sources, to mask minor
distracting sounds?   ___   ___   ___

Comments: _____

_____

11. Have the following elements been chosen to contribute
to noise reduction:

    a) Carpeting?   ___   ___   ___

    b) Floor surfaces that do not generate and/or
transfer noise?   ___   ___   ___

    c) Wall coverings?   ___   ___   ___

    d) Window coverings?   ___   ___   ___

    e) Ceiling surfaces?   ___   ___   ___

    f) Furniture?   ___   ___   ___

    g) Shelving?   ___   ___   ___

	YES	NO	N/A

h) Equipment? ____ ____ ____

*Comments:*_____

_____

D. Plumbing and Rest Rooms

1. Do all plumbing and rest-room facilities meet the
   ADA guidelines described earlier? ____ ____ ____
   *Comments:*_____

   _____

2. Are rest rooms constructed according to local
   building codes? ____ ____ ____
   *Comments:*_____

   _____

3. Are rest rooms and drinking fountains located near
   stairs, elevators, and other permanent installations? ____ ____ ____
   *Comments:*_____

   _____

4. Are rest rooms built above the level of the sewer system? ____ ____ ____
   *Comments:*_____

   _____

5. Does the number of sinks, toilets, and urinals meet
   local codes? ____ ____ ____
   *Comments:*_____

   _____

6. Does the design of the rest rooms accommodate one-
   third more toilets for women than men? ____ ____ ____
   *Comments:*_____

   _____

7. Are the toilets wall-hung to facilitate cleaning? ____ ____ ____
   *Comments:*_____

   _____

8. Are the toilets low-flow to conserve water? ____ ____ ____
   *Comments:*_____

   _____

	YES	NO	N/A

9. Have the best quality fixtures and accessories been selected?   ____ ____ ____

   *Comments:*_____

   _____

10. Does each rest room have a floor drain?   ____ ____ ____

    *Comments:*_____

    _____

11. Are the rest rooms:

    a) Well ventilated (including fans)?   ____ ____ ____

    b) Well lighted?   ____ ____ ____

    c) Soundproof?   ____ ____ ____

    d) Vandal proof, especially the wall and stall surfaces?   ____ ____ ____

    *Comments:*_____

    _____

12. Are there provisions for:

    a) Toilet paper?   ____ ____ ____

    b) Soap?   ____ ____ ____

    c) Trash receptacles?   ____ ____ ____

    d) Towel dispenser or hand dryers?   ____ ____ ____

    e) Sanitary napkin dispensers?   ____ ____ ____

    f) Other?   ____ ____ ____

    *Comments:*_____

    _____

13. Are dispensers mounted to accommodate a change of vendors without damaging wall surfaces?   ____ ____ ____

    *Comments:*_____

    _____

14. Are there shelves for holding books and papers?   ____ ____ ____

    *Comments:*_____

    _____

15. Is there lockable storage for supplies?   ____ ____ ____

	YES	NO	N/A

Comments:_____

_____

16. Are diaper-changing facilities available in all rest
    rooms?   ____   ____   ____

    Comments:_____

    _____

E. Elevators and Escalators

1. Are elevators/escalators located away from quiet
   areas?   ____   ____   ____

   Comments:_____

   _____

2. Are there separate elevators for the public, staff,
   and/or freight?   ____   ____   ____

   Comments:_____

   _____

3. Do elevators/escalators meet ADA codes?   ____   ____   ____

   Comments:_____

   _____

4. Do elevators/escalators meet all local codes? ____   ____   ____

   Comments:_____

   _____

5. Will the elevator/escalator system be designed so
   that routine maintenance will have minimal impact
   on library operations?   ____   ____   ____

   Comments:_____

   _____

Safety and Security

	YES	NO	N/A

A. General

1. Have all local codes regarding the safety of the occupants, building, and contents been met? ____ ____ ____

   *Comments:*_____
   _____

2. Do the security measures provide a benefit of increased customer and staff safety without projecting a negative "police state" image? ____ ____ ____

   *Comments:*_____
   _____

3. Do all alarm systems meet local codes when furnishings and decorations are in place? ____ ____ ____

   *Comments:*_____
   _____

4. If the building is located in an earthquake zone, are all seismic protection measures in place? ____ ____ ____

   *Comments:*_____
   _____

	YES	NO	N/A

B. External Security

1. Does the building require fencing to control access to the property?

   *Comments:*_____

2. Is there sufficient, tamper-proof security lighting?

   *Comments:*_____

3. Can access to roofs, upper windows, and ledges be gained by climbing trees, fences, the building structure, etc.?

   *Comments:*_____

4. Does the landscaping contribute to security by providing barriers to illegal entry?

   *Comments:*_____

5. Is landscaping designed to allow full visibility of facility and grounds?

   *Comments:*_____

6. Are all vulnerable access points (doors, windows, air vents, etc.) protected against illegal entry with:

   a) High-security locks and hinges?

   b) Security glazing?

   c) Barriers (fences, grilles)?

   d) Alarm systems?

   e) Lighting systems?

   *Comments:*_____

7. Does the intrusion alarm:

   a) Transmit to the police or security company?

   b) Immediately notify library personnel?

	YES	NO	N/A

    c) Have automatic reset? ____ ____ ____

    d) Have manual override? ____ ____ ____

    *Comments:*_____

_____

8. Are exterior book drops theft and tamper proof? ____ ____ ____

    *Comments:*_____

_____

C. Internal Security

1. Is there a materials theft-detection system? ____ ____ ____

    *Comments:*_____

_____

2. Does the alarm transmit to the circulation desk? ____ ____ ____

    *Comments:*_____

_____

3. Are windows and emergency exits wired to prevent
illegal use? ____ ____ ____

    *Comments:*_____

_____

4. Is there an emergency lighting system? ____ ____ ____

    *Comments:*_____

_____

5. Are all emergency exits clearly marked with lighted
signs? ____ ____ ____

    *Comments:*_____

_____

6. Are exhibits, rare-book collections, and other valuable
materials provided with secure rooms and/or cases? ____ ____ ____

    *Comments:*_____

_____

7. Is valuable equipment attached to fixtures with security
hardware? ____ ____ ____

    *Comments:*_____

_____

	YES	NO	N/A

8. Can patrons gain undetected access to nonpublic areas?   ____   ____   ____
   *Comments:*_____
   _____

9. Are there secluded areas that require convex mirrors
   or closed-circuit TV?   ____   ____   ____
   *Comments:*_____
   _____

10. Are there areas where patrons can be undetected at
    closing?   ____   ____   ____
    *Comments:*_____
    _____

11. Is there an after-hours motion-detector system in place?   ____   ____   ____
    *Comments:*_____
    _____

12. If the building has a security staff, is their desk/office
    in a prominent location in order to act as a deterrent?   ____   ____   ____
    *Comments:*_____
    _____

D. Fire Safety

1. Is the building protected by a fire-detection system,
   including smoke detectors?   ____   ____   ____
   *Comments:*_____
   _____

2. Are smoke detectors adequately distributed?   ____   ____   ____
   *Comments:*_____
   _____

3. Does the alarm transmit to a fire station or central
   alarm station?   ____   ____   ____
   *Comments:*_____
   _____

4. Are fire hoses and extinguishers adequately distributed
   and highly portable?   ____   ____   ____
   *Comments:*_____
   _____

	YES	NO	N/A

5. Is there a fire hydrant nearby?   ____   ____   ____
    *Comments:*_____
    _____

6. Is there a sprinkler system?   ____   ____   ____
    *Comments:*_____
    _____

7. Is shelving equipped with top panels to protect
    contents from water damage?   ____   ____   ____
    *Comments:*_____
    _____

8. Are there areas that require a special fire suppres-
    sion system:

    a) Multiple-level, open stacks?   ____   ____   ____

    b) Rare-book collections?   ____   ____   ____

    c) Computer room?   ____   ____   ____

    *Comments:*_____
    _____

Maintenance of Library Building and Property

	YES	NO	N/A

A. Graffiti

1. If graffiti occurs, is there a program in place to remove it as soon as possible? ___ ___ ___

   *Comments:*_____

2. Does the landscaping create a barrier to help protect against vandalism? ___ ___ ___

   *Comments:*_____

3. Are clinging vines used to cover walls to discourage graffiti? ___ ___ ___

   *Comments:*_____

4. Are planter boxes used to protect walls? ___ ___ ___

   *Comments:*_____

5. Will landscaping develop a dense mass against a wall so there is no room for graffiti? ___ ___ ___

   *Comments:*_____

	YES	NO	N/A

6. Is the building protected with a special coating or type of paint that allows for easy graffiti removal?

Comments: _____

_____

7. Does the concrete used have a dark color or pigmentation to discourage graffiti?

Comments: _____

_____

8. Is there security lighting to discourage graffiti?

Comments: _____

_____

9. Are the fixtures high enough on walls to protect them from vandalism?

Comments: _____

_____

10. Are signs high enough off the ground to protect them from vandalism?

Comments: _____

_____

11. Is masonry or stone being used to protect areas that are particularly vulnerable to graffiti?

Comments: _____

_____

12. Is the entrance secure from theft, vandalism, and graffiti?

Comments: _____

_____

13. Is the building well lit, with light directed toward vulnerable areas and walkways?

Comments: _____

_____

_____

B. Building Materials

1. Are exterior walls constructed of a durable and easily maintained material?

Comments: _____

_____

	YES	NO	N/A

2. Are windows built to help protect against direct sunlight and glare?

   *Comments:*_____

3. Can locally abundant building materials be used in the construction?

   *Comments:*_____

4. Are the materials used energy efficient?

   *Comments:*_____

5. Is the building constructed of fire-resistant materials?

   *Comments:*_____

6. Are the materials used of good quality?

   *Comments:*_____

7. Have natural colors and finishes been used and colors that would quickly become outdated been avoided?

   *Comments:*_____

8. Do the colors and finishes complement the character of the surrounding community?

   *Comments:*_____

C. Custodial Facilities

1. Is there adequate locking storage space allocated for janitorial supplies, tools, maintenance equipment, etc., on each floor?

   *Comments:*_____

2. Is a sink or running water available in the custodial room and is the floor sloped with a floor drain?

   *Comments:*_____

	YES	NO	N/A

3. Is the custodial room located as centrally as possible? ____ ____ ____

   *Comments:*_____

   _____

4. Is there a custodial clothes closet or locker? Does the door have a louver or vent? ____ ____ ____

   *Comments:*_____

   _____

5. Is there a mop, broom, and brush rack? ____ ____ ____

   *Comments:*_____

   _____

6. Is there a desk or worktable and tool storage area for minor repairs? ____ ____ ____

   *Comments:*_____

   _____

7. Is the door wide enough for ease of moving equipment in and out of the space? ____ ____ ____

   *Comments:*_____

   _____

8. Is the wall area around the sink of a durable material to prevent water damage? ____ ____ ____

   *Comments:*_____

   _____

D. Groundskeeper Facilities

1. Is there provision for secure storage of lawnmowers, snowblowers, and other equipment? ____ ____ ____

   *Comments:*_____

   _____

2. Is there provision for adequate outside faucets and electrical outlets? ____ ____ ____

   *Comments:*_____

   _____

3. Are faucets and electrical outlets vandal proof? ____ ____ ____

   *Comments:*_____

   _____

	YES	NO	N/A

E. Trash Enclosures

1. Is there adequate exterior space allocated for the storing of trash?

   _Comments:_____

2. Is the trash area easily accessible from the building and from the street for pickup?

   _Comments:_____

3. Is there adequate space allowed for garbage truck maneuvering and/or turnaround?

   _Comments:_____

4. Is the garbage bin hidden/camouflaged from public view with shrubs or a decorative wall?

   _Comments:_____

5. Is the area secure from scavenging?

   _Comments:_____

12

Building Occupancy and Post-Occupancy Evaluation

	YES	NO	N/A

A. Moving

1. Will the library employ a library-moving specialist, or will the library move with internal resources? ___ ___ ___

   *Comments:*_____

   _____

2. Can the move to the new space be scheduled during the time when demand for library services is at its lowest level of activity? ___ ___ ___

   *Comments:*_____

   _____

3. Will the library need to be closed in order to move to the new space? ___ ___ ___

   *Comments:*_____

   _____

4. If the library needs to close, how long can it remain open before it needs to be closed to move into the new space? ___ ___ ___

   *Comments:*_____

   _____

5. How much of the existing collection, stacks, furniture, and equipment will be moved to the new building? ___ ___ ___

   *Comments:*_____

   _____

	YES	NO	N/A

6. Has the amount to be moved been calculated and measured so that it will fit into the new space?

   *Comments:*_____

7. Will the items being moved be cleaned before the move?

   *Comments:*_____

8. Have timetables and schedules been made to plan all stages of the move?

   *Comments:*_____

B. Getting Ready for Occupancy

1. Will there be any organizational changes in the new building, and if so, have they been explained to staff?

   *Comments:*_____

2. Has the library's budget been adjusted to accommodate the new building (additional staff, utilities, etc.)?

   *Comments:*_____

3. Has all the furniture and equipment been ordered so that it will arrive when it is needed?

   *Comments:*_____

4. Will the library be required to change rules and regulations as a result of the new building?

   *Comments:*_____

5. Have VIP and staff tours been scheduled throughout the building process to get people involved and energized?

   *Comments:*_____

	YES	NO	N/A

6. Has a keying and access system been decided? ___ ___ ___
   Comments: _____
   _____

7. Has a room numbering system been decided? ___ ___ ___
   Comments: _____
   _____

8. Has the anticipated increased use of the facility
   been planned for? ___ ___ ___
   Comments: _____
   _____

C. Post-Occupancy Evaluation

1. Was the building completed on time? ___ ___ ___
   Comments: _____
   _____

2. Was the building completed within budget? ___ ___ ___
   Comments: _____
   _____

3. Were substantial change orders required? ___ ___ ___
   Comments: _____
   _____

4. Did the building meet the program? ___ ___ ___
   Comments: _____
   _____

5. Does the staff like the building, and if not, what
   can be changed to solve the problem? ___ ___ ___
   Comments: _____
   _____

6. Can the library maintain the building? ___ ___ ___
   Comments: _____
   _____

7. Did the architect provide all the services specified
   in his contract? ___ ___ ___
   Comments: _____
   _____

	YES	NO	N/A

8. Was the architect responsive to the needs of the client? ____ ____ ____
   *Comments:*_____

9. Did the architect adequately represent the client in negotiations with all of the publics? ____ ____ ____
   *Comments:*_____

10. Did the contractor adhere to his schedule? ____ ____ ____
    *Comments:*_____

11. Did the contractor maintain a clean and safe job site? ____ ____ ____
    *Comments:*_____

12. Did the contractor identify problems in the drawings and/or specifications during the project? ____ ____ ____
    *Comments:*_____

13. During the shakedown period (usually the one year warranty period after the building is accepted by the owner), were errors and/or omissions in the new building brought to the attention of the architect and contractor? ____ ____ ____
    *Comments:*_____

14. Were all errors and/or omissions resolved to the owner's satisfaction during the shakedown period? ____ ____ ____
    *Comments:*_____

13 ✓✓✓ Groundbreaking and Dedication Ceremonies

	YES	NO	N/A

A. Planning

1. Has planning begun at least three months before the scheduled event?

   *Comments:*_____

2. Have the key participants been informed of and agreed to the date and time of the event?

   *Comments:*_____

3. Are the date and time convenient to all of the people who may be interested in the event?

   *Comments:*_____

4. Are there any other events taking place in the community that may conflict with the event?

   *Comments:*_____

5. Have invitations to the event been sent out in a timely manner? (Allow at least one month before the event.)

   *Comments:*_____

	YES	NO	N/A

6. Has it been determined who will have a speaking
part at the event?

   *Comments:*_____

   _____

7. Has one person been designated to act as the coordi-
nator for the event?

   *Comments:*_____

   _____

8. Are devoted, talented people assigned to handle the
various jobs required to make the event successful?

   *Comments:*_____

   _____

9. Do all of the people working on the event know their
roles and responsibilities?

   *Comments:*_____

   _____

10. Has publicity been prepared and scheduled?

    *Comments:*_____

    _____

11. Have press releases been sent to the local media?

    *Comments:*_____

    _____

12. Have the media been contacted and urged to cover
the event?

    *Comments:*_____

    _____

13. Has a media contact person been identified
and listed in all publicity with their address and
telephone number?

    *Comments:*_____

    _____

14. Is there someone responsible for making an audio and
video history of the event?

    *Comments:*_____

    _____

15. Will the event be short, interesting, and focused?

    *Comments:*_____

    _____

	YES	NO	N/A

B. Event Checklist

1. Have street closures, parking, and traffic control been coordinated with the local law authorities? ___ ___ ___
   *Comments:*_____

2. Will the site be inspected and cleaned up before the event? ___ ___ ___
   *Comments:*_____

3. Will there be adequate signage indicating where attendees are to go? ___ ___ ___
   *Comments:*_____

4. For groundbreakings, will there be "ceremonial shovels" available? ___ ___ ___
   *Comments:*_____

5. For dedications, will there be "ceremonial scissors" available? ___ ___ ___
   *Comments:*_____

6. Has a source been found to provide:

   a) Tables? ___ ___ ___

   b) Chairs? ___ ___ ___

   c) Podium? ___ ___ ___

   d) Barricades? ___ ___ ___

   e) Public-address system? ___ ___ ___

   f) Stage? ___ ___ ___

   g) Flags? ___ ___ ___

   h) Refreshments? ___ ___ ___

   i) Tablecloths, napkins, plates, silverware, and cups? ___ ___ ___

   j) Trash cans/bags? ___ ___ ___

   k) Plants or decorations? ___ ___ ___

   l) Bathrooms and toilet supplies? ___ ___ ___

   *Comments:*_____

	YES	NO	N/A
7. Have all of the dignitaries been invited?	___	___	___
a) University or college administration?	___	___	___
b) Mayor?	___	___	___
c) City council?	___	___	___
d) Architect?	___	___	___
e) Contractor?	___	___	___
f) Project manager?	___	___	___
g) Friends of the Library?	___	___	___
h) Community groups?	___	___	___
i) Library VIPs?	___	___	___

*Comments:*_____

8. Will name tags be available?	___	___	___

*Comments:*_____

9. Will a guest book be available allowing event attendees to sign in?	___	___	___

*Comments:*_____

10. Have invitations been:			
a) Designed?	___	___	___
b) Printed?	___	___	___
c) Checked and checked again for accuracy?	___	___	___
d) Mailed at least one month before the event?	___	___	___
e) Copies saved for the library's archives?	___	___	___

*Comments:*_____

11. Has the program been:			
a) Designed?	___	___	___
b) Printed?	___	___	___

	YES	NO	N/A
c) Checked and checked again for accuracy?	___	___	___
d) Copies saved for the library's archives?	___	___	___

Comments:_____

_____

12. Will there be a master of ceremonies responsible for moderating the event?

	YES	NO	N/A
	___	___	___

Comments:_____

_____

13. Will speakers:

	YES	NO	N/A
a) Know and adhere to their time limit?	___	___	___
b) Provide the master of ceremonies with biographical information for introductions?	___	___	___
c) Provide copies of their remarks for the library's archives?	___	___	___
d) Know when to arrive and where to sit?	___	___	___
e) Know the proper attire to wear?	___	___	___

Comments:_____

_____

14. Has music been arranged for the event?

	YES	NO	N/A
	___	___	___

Comments:_____

_____

15. Will there be a color guard for a national anthem/ color ceremony?

	YES	NO	N/A
	___	___	___

Comments:_____

_____

16. If bad weather has the potential to affect the event, is there an alternative plan available?

	YES	NO	N/A
	___	___	___

Comments:_____

_____

17. Will thank-you letters be sent to:

	YES	NO	N/A
a) Donors?	___	___	___
b) Volunteers?	___	___	___
c) Friends?	___	___	___
d) Staff?	___	___	___

Comments:_____

_____

BIBLIOGRAPHY

Allen, Walter C. "Selected References." *Library Trends* 36, no. 2 (1987): 475–91.

Bahr, Alice Harrison. "Library Buildings in a Digital Age, Why Bother?" *C&RL News* 61, no. 7 (2000): 590–91.

Baumann, Charles H. *The Influence of Angus Snead Macdonald and the Snead Bookstack on Library Architecture.* Metuchen, N.J.: Scarecrow, 1972.

Bazillion, Richard J., and Connie Braun. 2d ed. *Academic Libraries as High-Tech Gateways.* Chicago: American Library Association, 2001.

Bernheim, Anthony. "San Francisco Main Library: A Healthy Building." Paper presented at the IFLA Council and Conference, Barcelona, Spain, August 25, 1993.

Black, J. B., Janet Black, Ruth O'Donnell, and Jane Scheuerle. *Surveying Public Libraries for the ADA.* Tallahassee: Bureau of Library Development, Division of Library and Information Services, State Library of Florida, 1993.

Boaz, Martha. *A Living Library: Planning Public Library Buildings for Cities of 100,000 or Less.* Los Angeles: University of Southern California Press, 1957.

Boss, Richard W. *Information Technologies and Space Planning for Libraries and Information Centers.* Boston: G. K. Hall, 1987.

____. *The Library Managers Guide to Automation.* 2d ed. White Plains: Knowledge Industry, 1984.

____. *Telecommunications for Library Management.* White Plains: Knowledge Industry, 1985.

Brawner, Lee, and Donald K. Beck Jr. *Determining Your Public Library's Future Size.* Chicago: American Library Association, 1996.

Breeding, Marshall. *Library LANs: Case Studies in Practice and Application.* Westport, Conn.: Meckler, 1992.

Brown, Carol R. *Selecting Library Furniture: A Guide for Librarians, Designers, and Architects.* Phoenix: Oryx, 1989.

California Library Association. *Earthquake Preparedness Manual for California Libraries.* Sacramento: California Library Association, 1990.

Carroll, R. E. "Building a Library: The Librarian/Architect Relationship." *New Zealand Libraries* 45 (March 1987): 85–89.

Ching, Francis D. K. *A Visual Dictionary of Architecture.* New York: Van Nostrand Reinhold, 1995.

Cohen, Elaine. "Library Facilities." *Bookmark* (spring 1990): 210–12.

____, and Aaron Cohen. *Designing and Space Planning for Libraries: A Behavioral Guide.* New York: Bowker, 1979.

Corban, Gaylan. E-mail, January 13, 1997.

Dahlgren, Anders C. "An Alternative to Library Building Standards." *Illinois Libraries* 67, no. 9 (November 1985): 772–77.

____. *Planning Library Buildings: A Select Bibliography.* Chicago: Library Administration and Management Association, ALA, 1990.

____. *Public Library Space Needs: A Planning Outline.* Madison: Wisconsin Department of Public Instruction, 1988.

Depew, John N. *A Library, Media, and Archival Preservation Handbook.* Santa Barbara: ABC-CLIO, 1991.

Dewe, Michael. *Library Buildings: Preparation for Planning Proceedings of the Seminar Held in Aberystwyth, August 10–14, 1987.* IFLA Publications #48. Munich, Germany: K. G. Saur, 1989.

Dublin, Fred. "Mechanical Systems in Libraries." *Library Trends* 36, no. 2 (fall 1987): 351–60.

Eckelman, Carl A., and Yusuf Z. Erdil. "Test Reports on 15 Models of Bracket-Type Steel Library Bookstacks." *Library Technology Reports* 34, no. 6 (1998): 685–786.

Fraley, Ruth A., and Carol Lee Anderson. *Library Space Planning: How to Assess, Allocate and*

Reorganize Collections, Resources, and Physical Facilities. New York: Neal-Schuman, 1990.

Gaines, Ervin, Marian Huttner, and Frances Peters. "Library Architecture: The Cleveland Experience." *Wilson Library Bulletin* 56, no. 8 (1982): 590–95.

Grant, Dorothy L., Thomas M. Grant, and Daniel S. Grant. *ADA Compliance Guidelines: California Access Code: Americans with Disabilities Act Title III: California Access Code Title 24.* San Diego: ACR Group, 1994.

Green, William R. *The Retail Store: Design and Construction.* New York: Van Nostrand Reinhold, 1991.

Habich, Elizabeth Chamberlain. *Moving Library Collections: A Management Handbook.* Ed. Gerard B. McCabe. Westport, Conn.: Greenwood, 1998.

Hagloch, Susan B. *Library Building Projects: Tips for Survival.* Englewood, Colo.: Libraries Unlimited, 1994.

Hawkins, Brian L., and Patricia Battin. *The Mirage of Continuity: Reconfiguring Academic Information Resources for the Twenty-First Century.* Washington, D.C.: Council on Library and Information Resources and Association of American Universities, 1998.

Henry, Karen H. *ADA: Ten Steps to Compliance.* Sacramento: California Chamber of Commerce, 1992.

Holt, Raymond M. *Planning Library Buildings and Facilities: From Concept to Completion.* Metuchen, N.J.: Scarecrow, 1989.

____. "Trends in Public Library Buildings." *Library Trends* 36, no. 2 (fall 1987): 267–85.

____, and Anders C. Dahlgren. *Wisconsin Library Building Project Handbook.* 2d ed. Madison: Department of Public Instruction, 1989.

Jones, Patrick. *Connecting Young Adults and Libraries: A How-to-Do-It Manual.* New York: Neal-Schuman, 1992.

Kirwin, William J. "What to Do Until the Architect Comes." *North Carolina Libraries* 39 (fall 1981): 5–8.

Klasing, Jane P. *Designing and Renovating School Library Media Centers.* Chicago: American Library Association, 1991.

Kolb, Audrey. *A Manual for Small Libraries.* 2d ed. Juneau: Alaska State Library, 1992.

Kroller, Franz. "Standards for Library Building." *Inspel* 16, no. 1 (1982): 40–44.

La Brec, Raymond. "Playing 20 Questions." *San Diego Daily Transcript*, November 16, 1999, 9A.

Langmead, Stephen. *New Library Design: Guidelines to Planning Academic Library Buildings.* Toronto: John Wiley Canada, 1970.

Leighton, Philip D., and David C. Weber. *Planning Academic and Research Library Buildings.* 3d ed. Chicago: American Library Association, 1999.

Lewis, Christopher. "The Americans with Disabilities Act and Its Effect on Public Libraries." *Public Libraries* (January/February 1992): 23–28.

Lewis, Myron E., and Mark L. Nelson. "How to Work with an Architect." *Wilson Library Bulletin* 57, no. 1 (1982): 44–46.

Library Administration and Management Association. *Library Buildings, Equipment and the ADA: Compliance Issues and Solutions.* Ed. Susan E. Cirillo and Robert E. Danford. Chicago: American Library Association, 1996.

Library of Michigan. *LSCA Builds Michigan Libraries.* Lansing: Library of Michigan, 1986.

Lushington, Nolan. "Getting It Right: Evaluating Plans in the Library Building Planning Process." *Library Administration & Management* 7, no. 3 (1993): 159–63.

____, and Willis N. Mills. *Libraries Designed for Users: A Planning Handbook.* Syracuse: Gaylord, 1979.

Martin, Ron G. *Libraries for the Future: Planning Buildings That Work: Proceedings of the Library Buildings Preconference, June 27–28, 1991, Atlanta, Georgia.* Chicago: American Library Association, 1992.

McCabe, Gerard B. *Operations Handbook for the Small Academic Library.* New York: Greenwood, 1989.

McCarthy, Richard C. *Designing Better Libraries: Selecting and Working with Building Professionals.* Fort Atkinson, Wisc.: Highsmith, 1995.

Merrill-Oldham, Jan, and Jutta Reed-Scott. "Library Storage Facilities, Management, and Services." In *Systems and Procedures Exchange Center,* compiled by Jan Merrill-Oldham and Jutta Reed-Scott, 2. Washington, D.C.: Association of Research Libraries, Office of Leadership and Management Services, 1999.

Mervis, Sybil Stern. "How to Plan a Groundbreaking Ceremony for the Library." *Illinois Libraries* 77, no. 3 (1995): 123–27.

Metcalf, Keyes D. *Planning Academic and Research Library Buildings.* New York: McGraw-Hill, 1965.

____. "Selection of Library Sites." *College & Research Libraries* 22 (May 1961): 183–92.

Michaels, Andrea. "Design Today." *Wilson Library Bulletin* 62, no. 8 (1988): 55–57.

Moore, Nick. *Measuring the Performance of Public Libraries.* Paris: UNESCO, 1989.

Mount, Ellis. *Creative Planning of Special Library Facilities.* New York: Haworth, 1988.

Natale, Joe. "Full and Equal Access: Americans with Disabilities Act." *Illinois Libraries* 73, no. 7 (1991): 599–602.

____. "The Next Step: The ADA Self-Evaluation." *Illinois Libraries* 74, no. 4 (1992): 284–91.

Novak, Gloria. "Movable Compact Shelving Systems: Selection and Specifications." *Library Technology Reports* 35, no. 5 (1999): 557–708.

Oxner, Sheldon R. *How to Select a Contractor.* Omaha: Simmons-Boardman, 1979.

Page, Kathryn. "Lighting Program for Libraries." Paper presented at the American Library Association Annual Conference, Chicago, 1995.

Pollet, D. "New Directions in Library Signage: You Can Get There from Here." *Wilson Library Bulletin* 50, no. 6 (1976): 456–62.

Rohlf, Robert H. "Best-Laid Plans: A Consultant's Constructive Advice." *School Library Journal* 36, no. 2 (February 1990): 28–31.

____. "New Factor in Planning Public Library Buildings." *Public Libraries* 26 (summer 1987): 52–53.

____. "The Selection of an Architect." *Public Libraries* 21, no. 1 (spring 1982): 5–8.

____, and David R. Smith. "Public Library Site Selection." *Public Libraries* 24, no. 2 (summer 1985): 47–49.

Sager, Don, ed. "Changing Perspectives: Joint Use of Facilities by Schools and Public Libraries." *Public Libraries* 38, no. 6 (1999): 355–59.

San Diego City. "Project Management Academy: The Executive Challenge, 2000." San Diego, Calif.: City of San Diego, 1994.

Sannwald, William W. *Event Checklist for Library Groundbreakings and Openings.* San Diego: San Diego Public Library, 1993.

____. *Mira Mesa Branch Library Building Program.* San Diego: San Diego Public Library, 1990.

Schott, Virginia O. "Site Selection for Rural Public Libraries." *Rural Libraries* 7, no. 2 (1987): 27–59.

Shelton, John A. *Seismic Safety Standards for Library Shelving, California State Library Manual of Recommended Practice.* Sacramento: California State Library Foundation, 1990.

Silver, Cy H. "Construction Standards for California Public Libraries." *Library Administration & Management* 4, no. 2 (1990): 82–86.

Simon, Matthew J., and George Yourke. "Building a Solid Architect-Client Relationship." *Library Administration & Management* 1 (June 1987): 100–104

Singh, Rajwant. "Standards and Specifications for Library Buildings." *Lucknow Librarian* 15, no. 2 (1983): 65–73.

Smith, Fran Kellogg, and Fred J. Bertolone. *Bringing Interiors to Light.* New York: Watson-Guptill, 1986.

Smith, Lester K. *Planning Library Buildings: From Decision to Design.* Chicago: American Library Association, 1986.

Strauch, Katina. "Selling Points: Shops in the Library." *Wilson Library Bulletin* 68, no. 6 (1994): 45–47.

Veatch, Lamar. "Toward the Environmental Design of Library Buildings." *Library Trends* 36, no. 2 (1987): 361–76.

Wheeler, Joseph, and Alfred Morton. *The American Public Library: Its Planning and Design with Special Reference to Its Administration and Service.* Chicago: American Library Association, 1941.

Winters, Willis C., and Brad Waters. "On the Verge of a Revolution: Current Trends in Library Lighting." *Library Trends* 36, no. 2 (1987): 327–59.

Wolf, Gary. "Exploring the Unmaterial World." *Wired* 8, no. 6 (2000): 308–19.

WILLIAM W. SANNWALD was director of the San Diego Public Library from 1979 to 1997. He currently is assistant to the city manager for library design and development and has been involved in the construction of over forty library buildings as either a consultant or owner's representative. He is the author of numerous books and articles on library architecture and management and has presented papers at national and international conferences. Past president of the Library Administration and Management Association (LAMA), Sannwald was a jury member of the joint ALA/AIA awards and chaired their award ceremony in 1995. He is the recipient of the San Diego AIA chapter's highest honor, the Irving Gill Award, for his contributions to library architecture.